GREAT COOKING MADE EASY

ORIENTAL RECIPES

Better Homes and Gardens
TRADEMARK

TREASURE PRESS

BETTER HOMES AND GARDENS BOOKS

Editor Gerald M. Knox
Art Director Ernest Shelton
Managing Editor David A. Kirchner
Project Editors James D. Blume, Marsha Jahns
Project Managers Liz Anderson, Jennifer Speer Ramundt, Angela K. Renkoski

Oriental Recipes (American edition)
Contributing Editor Lorene Frohling
Project Manager Marsha Jahns
Graphic Designer Lynda Haupert
Electronic Text Processor Donna Russell
Photographers Michael Jensen, Sean Fitzgerald
Food Stylists Suzanne Finley, Dianna Nolin, Janet Herwig, Maria Rolandelli

Oriental Recipes (British edition)
Project Managers Liz Anderson, Angela K. Renkoski
Assistant Art Director Harijs Priekulis
Contributing Project Editors Irena Chalmers Books, Inc., and associates: Jean Atcheson, Irena Chalmers, Ann Chase, Mary Dauman, Cathy Garvey, Mary Goodbody, Terri Griffing, Margaret Homberg, Kathryn Knapp, Stephanie Lyness, Susan Anderson Nabel, Victoria Proctor, Elizabeth Wheeler
Electronic Text Processors Alice Bauman, Kathy Benz, Paula Forest, Vicki Howell, Mary Mathews, Joyce Wasson

This edition first published in Great Britain in 1989 by:

Treasure Press
Michelin House
81 Fulham Road
London, SW3 6RB

Original edition published by Meredith Corporation in the United States of America.

BETTER HOMES AND GARDENS is a registered trademark in Canada, New Zealand, South Africa, and other countries.

ISBN 1 85051 433 X

Produced by Mandarin Offset
Printed and bound in Hong Kong

Oriental cooking—delicious, exciting, intriguing—is as much fun to create as it is to eat. It's a delightful food adventure filled with age-old cooking techniques and wonderful taste sensations.

Begin your culinary journey by browsing through *Oriental Recipes* for a sampling of the many specialities you've enjoyed in Oriental restaurants. Then, venture beyond the familiar to the extraordinary—sizzling satés, delicate steamed buns, delectable dim sum, and much, much more.

No need to worry about trying unfamiliar recipes, because we give you lots of help. We've fashioned the know-how of Oriental cooks into simple-to-follow directions throughout each chapter.

Puzzled by an unusual ingredient? Check our handy ingredient guide before you head for the market. Or, if you prefer to use a more common ingredient, try our practical suggestions for substitutes.

Contents

Oriental Roasting

Tender and succulent—
that's Oriental roasting at
its best. Now the centuries-
old secret of Oriental
roasting is yours with our
simple marinades.
Tantalisingly spiced, these
marinades transform pork
and poultry into delectable
dishes you'll often desire.

Turn the page, and
discover the captivating
taste of the Orient.

Oven-Roasted Spareribs

Oven-Roasted Spareribs

Buying Oriental ingredients in your supermarket is often easier than you think. But if you're unfamiliar with an ingredient, check the Special Helps (see pages 114–121) before you shop.

3   fluid ounces (80ml) soy sauce
2   tablespoons rice wine *or* dry sherry
2   tablespoons hoisin sauce
1   tablespoon cooking oil
1   teaspoon five-spice powder *or* Five-
       Spice Powder (see tip, page 11)
1   clove garlic, minced *
¼   teaspoon pepper
2   pounds (900g) pork loin back ribs
       or meaty spareribs, sawed in half
       across bones
4   fluid ounces (110ml) bottled plum
       sauce *or* Plum Sauce
       (see tip, page 11)
     Cucumber Sticks (optional)
       (see tip, opposite)
     Fresh cilantro *or* parsley (optional)

For marinade, in a small mixing bowl combine soy sauce, rice wine or dry sherry, hoisin sauce, oil, five-spice powder, garlic, and pepper.

Cut meat into single-rib portions. Trim separable fat from ribs. Place ribs in a polythene bag. Set the bag in a deep bowl. Pour marinade over ribs (see photo 1). Close the bag tightly and turn to coat ribs. Marinate in the refrigerator for 4 hours or overnight; turn the bag occasionally.

Line the bottom of a grill pan with foil. Top with a grill rack. Remove ribs from the bag and place, meaty side down, on the unheated rack (see photo 2). Set marinade aside. Roast ribs in a 375°F (190°C) gas mark 5 oven for 40 minutes or till no pink remains, turning and brushing twice with reserved marinade (see photo 3).

Brush with plum sauce. Turn ribs and brush again. Roast for 5 minutes more. To serve, arrange ribs on a serving dish. If desired, garnish with Cucumber Sticks and cilantro or parsley. Makes about 20 appetizer servings.

See cutting technique, page 27.

1 Pour the marinade over the meat in a polythene bag that's set in a deep bowl. The bowl makes moving the bag easier and reduces cleanup chores should the bag leak.

2 Transfer the meat from the polythene bag to the grill rack, letting the excess marinade drip back into the bag.

3 Brush the meat with the reserved marinade, using a basting brush. Basting keeps the meat moist as it roasts, and adds flavour, too.

Cucumber Sticks: Select a medium-size cucumber that has few or small seeds. Bias-slice the cucumber into ¼-inch (.5cm) slices, discarding the ends. Stack 3 or 4 slices together, then cut the stack into ¼-inch (.5cm) sticks, as shown. Stack and cut the remaining cucumber slices into sticks.

Chinese Roast Pork

Serve this Cantonese-style roast pork as a tasty appetizer. Add leftovers to fried rice (see recipe, page 38).

2   **fluid ounces (55ml) hoisin sauce**
2   **fluid ounces (55ml) soy sauce**
2   **tablespoons dry sherry**
2   **tablespoons honey**
1   **teaspoon grated root ginger***
1   **small clove garlic, minced***
½   **teaspoon five-spice powder *or* Five-Spice Powder (see tip, opposite)**
3   **pound (1kg350g) loin of pork**
    Hot Mustard Sauce, bottled plum sauce, *or* Plum Sauce (see tip, opposite) (optional)
    Toasted Sesame Seed (optional)

For marinade, in a small mixing bowl combine hoisin sauce, soy sauce, dry sherry, honey, root ginger, garlic, and five-spice powder; set aside.

Trim bone and separable fat from pork. Cut pork crosswise into 1-inch (2.5cm)-thick slices. Place pork slices in a polythene bag. Set the bag in a deep bowl. Pour marinade over pork (see photo 1, page 8). Close the bag tightly and turn to coat pork. Marinate in the refrigerator for 6 hours or overnight, turning occasionally. Meanwhile, prepare Hot Mustard Sauce or Plum Sauce, and Toasted Sesame Seed, if desired.

Line the bottom of a grill pan with foil. Top with a grill rack. Remove pork from the bag and place on the unheated rack (see photo 2, page 8). Set marinade aside. Roast pork in a 350°F (180°C) gas mark 4 oven for 30 to 35 minutes or until no pink remains, turning and brushing occasionally with reserved marinade (see photo 3, page 9).

Cut pork into thin strips; sprinkle with Toasted Sesame Seed, if desired. Serve with sauce for dipping, if desired. Makes about 16 appetizer servings or 1¼ pounds (560g) meat.

Hot Mustard Sauce: In a small mixing bowl combine 2 ounces (50g) *mustard powder* and 1

See cutting technique, page 27.

teaspoon *sesame oil* or *cooking oil*. (*Or*, for a spicier sauce, substitute ½ teaspoon *chilli oil* or *Chilli Oil* [see tip, opposite].) Gradually stir in 3 tablespoons *water*. Serve at room temperature. Makes about 2 ounces (50g).

Toasted Sesame Seed: Spread *sesame seed* in thin layer in shallow baking tin. Bake in 350°F (180°C) gas mark 4 oven 7 to 10 minutes or until light brown, stirring once or twice.

Chicken in Soy Sauce

An Indonesian dish spiced with a sweet soy marinade.

1   **large onion, finely chopped (5 ounces or 150g)**
2   **cloves garlic, minced***
1   **tablespoon Oriental chilli paste**
2   **tablespoons cooking oil**
3   **fluid ounces (80ml) lemon juice**
2   **fluid ounces (55ml) sweet soy sauce *or* Sweet Soy Sauce (see tip, opposite)**
1   **2½- to 3-pound (1kg125g to 1kg350g) chicken, cut up**

For marinade, in a medium frying pan cook onion, garlic, and chilli paste in hot oil till onion is tender but not brown. Remove from heat; stir in lemon juice and sweet soy sauce. Cool.

Meanwhile, rinse chicken, then pat dry. Place chicken in a polythene bag. Set the bag in a deep bowl. Pour marinade over chicken (see photo 1, page 8). Close the bag tightly and turn to coat chicken. Marinate in the refrigerator for 4 hours or overnight, turning occasionally.

Line bottom of a grill pan with foil. Top with lightly greased grill rack. Remove chicken from bag and place on unheated rack (see photo 2, page 8). Set marinade aside. Roast chicken in a 375°F (190°C) gas mark 5 oven for 40 to 45 minutes or until tender; turn and brush occasionally with reserved marinade (see photo 3, page 9). Transfer to serving dish; garnish with lemon twists, if desired. Makes 6 servings.

Homemade Ingredients

Sometimes Oriental cooking and unfamiliar ingredients seem to go hand in hand. To avoid searching for some of these unusual ingredients, use our easy-to-make homemade recipes as substitutes for similar commercial products. These recipes make use of readily available ingredients and take little time to prepare in your kitchen.

Sesame Paste

In a food processor bowl or blender container place 6 ounces (175g) *sesame seed*. Cover and process or blend to a fine powder. Through the hole in the lid or with the lid ajar, gradually add 2 tablespoons *cooking oil,* processing or blending till mixture is smooth. Cover and store in the refrigerator. Makes about 4 ounces (110g).

Plum Sauce

In a small saucepan combine 12 ounces (350g) *plum preserves;* 2 tablespoons *vinegar;* 1 tablespoon *soft brown sugar;* 1 tablespoon finely chopped *onion;* 1 teaspoon seeded and finely chopped dried *red chilli pepper* (see Note, page 30) *or* 1 teaspoon crushed *red pepper;* 1 clove *garlic,* minced;* and ½ teaspoon ground *ginger*. Bring to the boil, stirring constantly. Remove from heat; cover and chill overnight. Makes 10 fluid ounces (275ml).

Chilli Oil

In a small saucepan heat 3 fluid ounces (80ml) *cooking oil** and 2 tablespoons *sesame oil* to 365°F (185°C). Remove from heat. Stir in 2 teaspoons ground *red pepper*. Cool. Strain. Cover and store in the refrigerator. Makes about 4 fluid ounces (110ml).
Note: For milder flavour, increase *cooking oil* to 4 fluid ounces (110ml).

Sweet Soy Sauce

In a heavy 10-inch (25.5cm) frying pan heat 9 ounces (250g) *caster sugar* over medium heat till it begins to melt, without stirring. Once the sugar begins to melt, cook and stir for 2 to 3 minutes or till golden. Remove from heat.

Slowly and carefully stir in 6 fluid ounces (165ml) *water;* 6 fluid ounces (165ml) *soy sauce;* and 1 *star anise,* finely crushed, *or* 1 teaspoon *aniseed*. (Watch for spattering.) Return the frying pan to the heat. Bring to the boil; reduce heat. Simmer about 15 minutes or till mixture is slightly thickened and sugar is dissolved, stirring constantly. Cool to room temperature.

Skim off foam and any anise that floats to the top. Strain to remove additional anise. Cover and store in the refrigerator. Makes about 11 fluid ounces (300ml).

Dried Tangerine Peel

Using a vegetable peeler, thinly slice peel from 3 *tangerines or oranges* into 1½x½-inch (4x1cm) strips; scrape off excess white membrane. Place tangerine or orange strips in a single layer on a baking sheet.

Bake in a 300°F (150°C) gas mark 2 oven till strips are dried. Allow 7 to 10 minutes for tangerine peel and 10 to 12 minutes for orange peel. Store dried peel in a covered container. Makes about 3 ounces (75g).

Five-Spice Powder

In a small mixing bowl combine 1 teaspoon ground *cinnamon;* 1 *star anise,* finely crushed, *or* 1 teaspoon *aniseed;* ¼ teaspoon *fennel seed,* crushed; ¼ teaspoon whole *Szechwan peppers or* whole *black peppers,* crushed; and ⅛ teaspoon ground *cloves*. Store mixture in a covered container. Makes 2 teaspoons.

Red-Cooking

Often overlooked and underrated, red-cooking deserves equal billing with stir-frying as truly authentic Chinese cooking.

Red-cooking simmers food in a spicy soy sauce stock, imparting a rich, robust flavour. As the name suggests, the well-seasoned stock also adds a very handsome reddish-brown colour to the food.

Give this Chinese speciality centre stage at mealtime, and enjoy the applause.

Red-Cooked Chicken

Red-Cooked Chicken

3 tablespoons dried tangerine peel *or*
  Dried Tangerine Peel (see tip, page 11)
1 tablespoon whole Szechwan peppers *or*
  whole black peppers
3 inches (7.5cm) stick cinnamon
1 star anise *or* 1 teaspoon aniseed
24 fluid ounces (680ml) water
8 fluid ounces (220ml) soy sauce
4 fluid ounces (110ml) rice wine *or* dry
  sherry
4 spring onions, cut into 1-inch (2.5cm)
  pieces
3 tablespoons soft brown sugar
1 2½- to 3-pound (1kg125g to 1kg350g)
  chicken
  Carrot Flowers (optional) (see tip,
  right)

For spice bag, wrap tangerine peel, Szechwan or black peppers, cinnamon, and star anise *or aniseed in cheesecloth (see photo 1). In a large covered casserole mix water, soy sauce, rice wine or dry sherry, spring onion pieces, brown sugar, and spice bag. Bring to the boil.

Rinse chicken. Place in soy sauce mixture, breast side down. Spoon soy sauce mixture over chicken (see photo 2). Return to boiling; reduce heat. Cover and simmer for 25 minutes.

Turn chicken. Baste again with cooking liquid. Simmer, covered, 25 to 30 minutes more or until meat is tender, basting often last 10 minutes.

Transfer chicken to a serving dish; reserve cooking liquid. If desired, garnish chicken with Carrot Flowers and *spring onion slivers*. Strain reserved liquid (see photo 3). Skim fat from liquid. Store liquid in the refrigerator for up to 3 days or in the freezer for up to 6 months. Reuse for other red-cooked dishes. Makes 6 servings.

Red-Cooked Young Pigeons *or* Cornish Game Hens: Prepare Red-Cooked Chicken as above, *except* substitute four 12- to 14-ounce (350 to 400g) *young pigeons* or two 1- to 1½-pound (450 to 700g) *Cornish game hens* for

See cutting technique, page 27.

chicken. Reduce the first cooking time to 20 minutes. Turn and baste (see photo 2). Simmer, covered, until tender, basting often during the last 10 minutes. Allow 15 to 20 minutes for pigeons and 20 to 25 minutes for hens. Serve pigeons whole or halve hens lengthwise. If desired, garnish as above. Makes 4 servings.

1 Place the spices on a double layer of cheesecloth. Gather the cloth edges together over the spices, as shown. Tie with string.

2 Using a large spoon, baste the food with the soy sauce mixture. Basting adds flavour, colour, and moisture to the surface of the food.

Carrot Flowers: Cut 1 large carrot into 2- to 3-inch (5 to 7.5cm) lengths. For each section, make a lengthwise cut ¼-inch (.5cm) deep. Cut again at an angle to the first cut to form a V-shaped wedge; remove the wedge. Cut 3 more wedges around the carrot. Cut carrot into ⅛- to ¼-inch (3mm to .5cm) slices.

3 Drape a double layer of cheesecloth over a sieve placed in a large bowl. To strain the red-cooking liquid, pour it through the sieve, as shown. Then, discard the spice bag.

Savoury Soups

Hot soup is as much a mealtime staple in the Orient as the ever-present rice bowl. Traditionally, the soup is brought to the table in a communal pot, and all those around the table serve themselves throughout the meal.

Refreshing Far Eastern soups both quench the diners' thirsts and add savoury flavour to meals.

Spicy Chicken Soup

Spicy Chicken Soup

Made with rice sticks, this Southeast Asian soup is seasoned with a spice blend reminiscent of curry. If you don't have rice sticks, use cooked spaghetti or fine egg noodles as a substitute.

1   **ounce (25g) rice sticks**
    Fried Onion Flakes (see tip, opposite)
1   **whole medium chicken breast (about 12 ounces [350g]), skinned and boned (see tip, page 34)**
½   **teaspoon ground coriander**
½   **teaspoon shrimp paste *or* anchovy paste**
¼   **teaspoon ground turmeric**
¼   **teaspoon ground cumin**
2   **tablespoons water**
1   **medium onion, chopped (4 ounces [110g])**
2   **tablespoons finely chopped macadamia nuts *or* blanched almonds**
1   **clove garlic, minced***
1   **teaspoon grated root ginger***
1   **tablespoon cooking oil**
1½ **pints plus 2 fluid ounces (900ml) chicken broth**
2   **teaspoons lemon juice**
1   **medium potato, peeled, cooked, and chopped**
1   **hard-boiled egg, coarsely chopped**
2   **spring onions, thinly sliced**

In a medium mixing bowl soak rice sticks in enough hot water to cover for 30 minutes. Drain well. Cut rice sticks into 3-inch (7.5cm) lengths (see photo 1). Set aside. Prepare Fried Onion Flakes. Cut chicken into bite-size pieces.

In a small mixing bowl combine coriander, shrimp paste or anchovy paste, turmeric, and cumin; gradually stir in water. In a large saucepan cook chopped onion, macadamia nuts or almonds, garlic, and root ginger in hot oil over medium-high heat for 3 to 4 minutes or until onion is tender but not brown, stirring often.

Add coriander mixture; cook and stir for 1 minute. Add broth and chicken; bring to the boil. Reduce heat; cover and simmer for 5 minutes (see photo 2).

Add rice sticks. Cook, uncovered, for 5 minutes, stirring occasionally. Add lemon juice. Divide potato, hard-boiled egg, and spring onions among 4 soup bowls. Top with broth mixture (see photo 3). Sprinkle with *2 to 3 teaspoons* of the Fried Onion Flakes. Makes 4 servings.

1 After soaking and draining the rice sticks, cut them into 3-inch (7.5cm) lengths, using a sharp knife. Use the same technique for cutting bean threads.

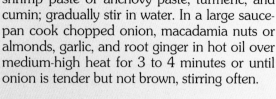

Fried Onion Flakes:
Stir 1½ ounces (40g) dried minced *onion* in 1 tablespoon hot *cooking oil* over medium heat for 3 to 4 minutes or till golden brown. Drain on kitchen paper. Cool. Store in the refrigerator. Sprinkle over soups and salads. Makes 1½ ounces (40g).

2 As the broth mixture begins to boil, reduce the heat to simmer, and cover the saucepan. Gentle simmering enhances the flavour of the soup.

3 Ladle the soup from the saucepan into individual soup bowls and serve immediately. Unlike most soups, Spicy Chicken Soup is served *over* the garnishes, as shown.

Hot and Sour Prawn Soup

12 ounces (350g) fresh *or* frozen medium
    prawns in shells
2 stalks lemongrass
1 tablespoon cooking oil
32 fluid ounces (900ml) chicken broth
    Lemon peel (about 2x1-inch [5x2.5cm]
    rectangle), cut into strips
    Lime peel (about 1-inch [2.5cm]
    square), cut into strips
1 green chilli *or* jalapeño pepper, seeded
    and chopped (see Note, page 30)
1 spring onion, thinly sliced
1 tablespoon lime juice
2 teaspoons fish sauce
    Snipped fresh cilantro *or* parsley
1 red *or* green chilli pepper, seeded and
    finely chopped (optional)

Thaw prawns, if frozen; rinse. Peel and devein (see page 21), reserving shells (see tip, opposite). Halve prawn lengthwise; set aside. Discard outer layers of lemongrass; cut stalks into 1-inch (2.5cm) pieces.

In a large saucepan cook reserved prawn shells in hot oil over medium-high heat till shells turn pink, stirring often. Add lemongrass, chicken broth, lemon peel, lime peel, and 1 chilli or jalapeño pepper. Bring mixture to the boil. Reduce heat; cover and simmer for 20 minutes (see photo 2, page 19).

Strain broth through a sieve lined with cheesecloth (see photo 3, page 15). Return broth to saucepan; bring to the boil. Add prawns. Return to the boil; reduce heat and simmer, uncovered, for 1 to 2 minutes or till prawns turn pink, stirring occasionally.

Stir in spring onion, lime juice, and fish sauce; heat for 1 minute. Ladle into soup bowls (see photo 3, page 19). Garnish with cilantro or parsley and red or green chilli pepper, if desired. Makes 4 servings.

*See cutting technique, page 27.

Korean Beef Soup

6 ounces (175g) cooked beef
1 medium onion, chopped (2 ounces
    [50g])
1 tablespoon sesame oil *or* cooking oil
2 cloves garlic, minced*
1 teaspoon grated root ginger*
1 to 2 teaspoons Korean chilli sauce *or*
    hot bean paste, *or* ½ teaspoon
    ground red pepper
32 fluid ounces (900ml) beef broth
4 ounces (110g) fresh bean sprouts
1 medium carrot, cut into julienne strips
    Spring onion slivers*

Cut beef into matchstick-size shreds (see tip, page 35). In a large saucepan cook onion in hot sesame oil or cooking oil over medium-high heat for 2 minutes, stirring often.

Stir in garlic; root ginger; and chilli sauce, hot bean paste, or red pepper. Cook and stir about 1 minute or until onion is tender but not brown. Add beef broth; bring mixture to the boil. Stir in beef shreds, bean sprouts, and carrot strips; return to the boil. Reduce heat; cover and simmer for 10 minutes (see photo 2, page 19). Ladle into soup bowls (see photo 3, page 19). Top with spring onion. Makes 4 servings.

Dashi

34 fluid ounces (955ml) water
1 3½-inch (8.5cm) square dried kelp
    (konbu)
½ ounce (10g) dried bonito flakes
    (katsuo-bushi)

In a medium saucepan bring water and kelp to the boil; immediately remove kelp. Stir in bonito flakes. Remove from heat; let stand for 2 minutes. Strain through a sieve lined with cheesecloth (see photo 3, page 15). Store in the refrigerator for up to 3 days. (Do not freeze.) Use Dashi as directed in recipe. Makes about 32 fluid ounces (900ml).

Chicken and Vegetable Soup

Check the Special Helps section for more information on miso and other ingredients that may be new to you.

1½ **pints (195ml) Dashi (see recipe, opposite)**
 1 **whole small chicken breast (about 8 ounces [225g]), skinned and boned (see tip, page 34)**
 2 **fluid ounces (55ml) white miso**
 4 **ounces (110g) taro root, peeled and thinly sliced**
 4 **ounces (110g) daikon, peeled and cut into julienne strips**
 1 **carrot, thinly sliced**
 1 **teaspoon grated root ginger**
 ¼ **teaspoon salt**
 4 **ounces (110g) tofu (fresh bean curd), cut into ½-inch (1cm) cubes**
 2 **ounces (50g) torn fresh spinach**

Prepare Dashi; set aside. Cut chicken breast into bite-size pieces.

In a large saucepan combine Dashi and miso. Stir in chicken pieces, taro root, daikon, carrot, root ginger, and salt. Bring mixture to the boil. Reduce heat; cover and simmer for 12 minutes (see photo 2, page 19).

Add tofu and spinach. Cook, uncovered, for 2 minutes, stirring occasionally. Ladle into soup bowls (see photo 3, page 19). Makes 4 servings.

Cleaning Prawns

Peeling
Starting near the head end, use your fingers to open and peel back the shell on the underside of the prawn. Then, pull on the tail portion of the shell and remove it.

Deveining
Make a shallow slit along the back of the prawn. If the black sand vein is visible, use the tip of the knife to remove it. Then, rinse the prawn under cold running water.

Stir-Fry Cooking

Stir-frying—quick, simple, and exciting. This age-old Oriental cooking method is easy. Simply follow our step-by-step photos and you'll soon be able to cook like a pro.

Start with a wok or a large frying pan. Assemble all the ingredients, then cut, slice, dice, or mince them. Toss everything in the pan, stir a bit, and in a flash you've created a sizzling, crisp-tender stir-fry.

Broccoli in Oyster Sauce

Broccoli in Oyster Sauce

8	dried mushrooms
12	ounces (350g) fresh broccoli
4	spring onions
1	clove garlic
	Root ginger
3	fluid ounces (80ml) chicken broth
1	to 2 tablespoons oyster sauce
1	teaspoon cornflour
1	teaspoon caster sugar
1	tablespoon cooking oil

In a small mixing bowl soak mushrooms in enough hot water to cover for 30 minutes. Rinse well and squeeze to drain thoroughly. Slice thinly, discarding stems; set aside.

Cut broccoli florets into bite-size pieces. Halve any large broccoli stems lengthwise; roll-cut stems into ¾-inch (2cm) pieces.* In a medium saucepan cook stems, covered, in a small amount of boiling water for 2 minutes. Add florets; cook for 1 minute more. Drain.

Bias-slice spring onions into 1-inch (2.5cm) pieces.* Mince garlic.* Grate 1 teaspoon root ginger.* For sauce, in a small mixing bowl combine chicken broth, oyster sauce, cornflour, and sugar; set aside.

Preheat a wok or large frying pan over high heat; add oil (see photo 1). Stir-fry garlic and root ginger in hot oil for 15 seconds (see photo 2). Add broccoli and mushrooms; stir-fry for 3 minutes (see photo 3). Add spring onions; stir-fry for 1½ to 2 minutes or until all vegetables are crisp-tender. Push from the centre of the wok.

Stir sauce; add to the centre of the wok or frying pan (see photo 4). Cook and stir until thickened and bubbly. Cook and stir for 1 minute more. Stir in vegetables to coat with sauce. Makes 4 servings.

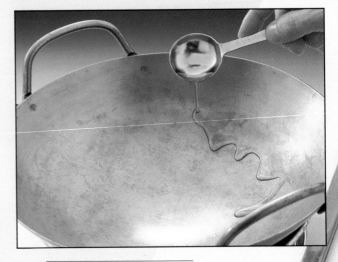

1 Add the oil in a ring around the upper part of the wok so that it coats the sides as it runs down. Or, add the oil to a frying pan; tilt it to coat the bottom.

2 Stir-fry the seasonings in the hot oil so that the oil is flavoured before the vegetables are added. Stir constantly to prevent the seasonings from burning.

*See cutting technique, page 27.

3 Using a wok spatula or a long-handled spoon in each hand, lift and turn the vegetables constantly. Stir-frying cooks the food quickly and evenly.

4 With the vegetables pushed up the side of the wok, add the sauce mixture to the centre of the hot wok. Immediately stir the sauce to keep lumps from forming.

Szechwan Stir-Fried Cabbage

Whole chilli peppers add fire to the cabbage as it cooks, but remember to remove them before serving.

1 **medium head Chinese cabbage**
1 **teaspoon whole Szechwan peppers *or* whole black peppers**
  Root ginger
2 **tablespoons soy sauce**
1 **tablespoon dry sherry**
2 **teaspoons rice vinegar *or* vinegar**
1 **teaspoon cornflour**
1 **teaspoon caster sugar**
1 **tablespoon sesame oil *or* cooking oil**
4 **dried red chilli peppers**

Chop cabbage into 2-inch (5cm) pieces. Crush Szechwan or black peppers. Grate 1 teaspoon root ginger.* For sauce, in a small mixing bowl combine soy sauce, dry sherry, rice vinegar or vinegar, cornflour, and sugar; set aside.

Preheat a wok or large frying pan over high heat; add oil (see photo 1, page 24). Stir-fry whole chilli peppers and crushed pepper in hot oil about 1 minute or till chilli peppers turn dark (see photo 2, page 24). Push peppers from the centre of the wok. Add root ginger; stir-fry for 15 seconds. Add cabbage; stir-fry for 3 minutes (see photo 3, page 25). Push cabbage mixture from centre of the wok.

Stir sauce; add to the centre of the wok or frying pan (see photo 4, page 25). Cook and stir till thickened and bubbly. Cook and stir for 1 minute more. Stir in cabbage mixture to coat with sauce. Remove chilli peppers. Makes 4 servings.

Bean Sprouts With Carrots

4 **small carrots**
4 **small spring onions**
2 **cloves garlic**
  Root ginger
3 **tablespoons chicken broth *or* water**
2 **tablespoons rice wine *or* dry sherry**
½ **teaspoon cornflour**
½ **teaspoon caster sugar**
¼ **teaspoon salt**
1 **tablespoon cooking oil**
8 **ounces (225g) fresh bean sprouts**

Bias-slice carrots into ¼-inch (.5cm) pieces.* Roll-cut spring onions into 1-inch (2.5cm) pieces.* Mince garlic.* Grate 1 teaspoon root ginger.* For sauce, in a small mixing bowl combine chicken broth or water, rice wine or dry sherry, cornflour, sugar, and salt; set aside.

Preheat a wok or large frying pan over high heat; add oil (see photo 1, page 24). Stir-fry garlic and root ginger in hot oil for 15 seconds (see photo 2, page 24). Add carrots; stir-fry for 3 to 4 minutes or till almost crisp-tender (see photo 3, page 25). Add spring onions; stir-fry for 1 minute. Add bean sprouts. Push vegetables from the centre of the wok.

Stir sauce; add to the centre of the wok or frying pan (see photo 4, page 25). Cook and stir till thickened and bubbly. Cook and stir for 1 minute more. Stir in vegetables to coat with sauce. Makes 4 servings.

See cutting technique, page 27.

Cutting Vegetables

Roll Cutting
Hold broccoli stem or other vegetable at a 45-degree angle to a cleaver or a sharp knife for the first cut. Give the stem a half-turn, then cut again at the same angle as the first cut, as shown.

Bias Slicing
Hold leek or other vegetable at a 45-degree angle to a cleaver or a sharp knife for the first cut. Make each succeeding cut at the same angle as the first cut, spacing the cuts evenly, as shown.

Julienne Cutting
Cut vegetable into 2-inch (5cm) lengths, using a cleaver or knife. Cut each section lengthwise into ¼-inch (.5cm)-thick slices. Stack a few slices together, then cut lengthwise to make thin strips, as shown.

Slivering
Cut spring onion into 2-inch (5cm) lengths, using a cleaver or a sharp knife. Halve each section lengthwise. (Quarter larger onions lengthwise.) Then, cut each section lengthwise into thin slivers or strips, as shown.

Mincing
Place unpeeled garlic cloves on a cutting board. Using the side of your fist, pound the flat side of a cleaver or a wide-blade knife against the garlic. Remove the peel, then very finely chop the garlic with an up-and-down chopping motion, as shown.

Grating
Hold unpeeled root ginger or other food at a 45-degree angle to a fine grater. Move the root ginger back and forth across the grating surface, as shown. Wrap the unused root ginger in kitchen paper. Store in the refrigerator.

House Specialities From the Wok

Palate pleasing, colourful, and diverse, stir-frys are the most popular entrées on a Chinese restaurant menu.

In this section we've selected our favourite Cantonese, Peking, and Szechwan stir-frys. Each recipe gives you a just-right balance of flavours.

These dishes are sure to become specialities at your house, too.

Beef and Peppers in Black Bean Sauce

Beef and Peppers In Black Bean Sauce

A Cantonese favourite you'll enjoy at home.

1 **pound (450g) beef sirloin**
1 **slightly beaten egg white**
1 **tablespoon water**
2 **teaspoons cornflour**
2 **teaspoons soy sauce**
5 **spring onions**
1 **large green pepper**
2 **tablespoons fermented black beans**
2 **cloves garlic**
4 **fluid ounces (110ml) water**
2 **tablespoons soy sauce**
1 **tablespoon dry sherry**
2 **teaspoons cornflour**
1 **tablespoon cooking oil**
  Red chilli pepper, seeded and thinly
    sliced (optional)
  Chilli Pepper Flower (optional)
    (see tip, right)

Partially freeze beef; bias-slice across the grain into bite-size strips (see tip, page 35). For marinade, in a medium mixing bowl combine egg white, 1 tablespoon water, 2 teaspoons cornflour, and 2 teaspoons soy sauce; stir in beef. Cover and let stand at room temperature for 30 minutes, stirring occasionally. (*Or,* marinate in the refrigerator for 2 hours.)

Bias-slice spring onions into 1-inch (2.5cm) pieces.* Seed and cut green pepper into 1-inch (2.5cm) squares. Rinse beans; chop finely. Mince garlic.* For sauce, in a small mixing bowl combine 4 fluid ounces (110ml) water, 2 tablespoons soy sauce, dry sherry, and 2 teaspoons cornflour; set aside.

(See stir-frying photos, pages 24–25.) Preheat a wok or large frying pan over high heat; add oil. (Add more oil as necessary during cooking.) Stir-fry beans and garlic in hot oil for 15 seconds or till fragrant. Add spring onions and green pepper; stir-fry about 1½ minutes or until crisp-

*See cutting technique, page 27.

tender. Remove vegetables (see photo 1). Add *half* of the beef to the hot wok or frying pan (see photo 2). Stir-fry for 2 to 3 minutes or until done. Remove beef. Stir-fry remaining beef for 2 to 3 minutes or until done. Return all beef to the wok. Push from the centre of the wok.

Stir sauce; add to the centre of the wok or frying pan. Cook and stir until thickened and bubbly. Return vegetables to the wok; stir ingredients together to coat with sauce (see photo 3). Cook and stir for 1 minute more. If desired, garnish with sliced chilli pepper and Chilli Pepper Flower. Makes 4 servings.

Chilli Pepper Flower: Cut a red chilli pepper in half, cutting to, but not through, the stem end; discard seeds. Cut each half into strips, leaving stem end whole. Place pepper in ice water about 30 minutes or until the ends curl; drain.
Note: Always wear plastic or rubber gloves to protect your skin from the oils in the pepper. Avoid direct contact with your eyes. When finished, wash your hands thoroughly.

1 Using wok spatulas, transfer the stir-fried vegetables from the wok to a mixing bowl. Set the vegetables aside while you stir-fry the meat.

2 Add the meat to the wok *half* at a time unless the recipe directs otherwise. This prevents overloading the wok and slowing the cooking when you are stir-frying.

3 After cooking the sauce, return the vegetables to the wok. Then, stir all of the ingredients together, as shown. This final stirring evenly distributes the sauce and makes certain everything is hot.

Kung Pao Chicken

To prevent sticking, use a vigorous stir-frying action whenever egg white is used in the marinade, as in this spicy Szechwan dish.

  2 **whole medium chicken breasts
       (about 1½ pounds [700g] total),
       skinned and boned**
  1 **slightly beaten egg white**
  2 **tablespoons cornflour**
  1 **teaspoon dry sherry**
  1 **teaspoon soy sauce**
  4 **spring onions**
  8 **ounces (225g) tinned water chestnuts,
       drained**
  1 **clove garlic**
  2 **tablespoons dry sherry**
  2 **tablespoons rice vinegar *or* vinegar**
  2 **tablespoons soy sauce**
  1 **tablespoon caster sugar**
  2 **teaspoons cornflour**
  1 **to 2 teaspoons Oriental chilli paste**
  2 **tablespoons cooking oil**
  4 **ounces (110g) tinned bamboo shoots,
       drained**
1½ **ounces (40g) unsalted dry roasted
       peanuts**
  1 **teaspoon sesame oil (optional)**

Cut chicken breasts into ½-inch (1cm) cubes (see tip, page 35). For marinade, in a medium mixing bowl combine beaten egg white, 2 tablespoons cornflour, 1 teaspoon dry sherry, and 1 teaspoon soy sauce; stir in cubed chicken. Cover and let stand at room temperature for 30 minutes, stirring occasionally. (*Or,* marinate in the refrigerator for 2 hours.)

Meanwhile, bias-slice spring onions into ½-inch (1cm) pieces.* Coarsely chop drained water chestnuts. Mince garlic.* Set all aside.

For sauce, in a small mixing bowl combine 2 tablespoons dry sherry, rice vinegar or vinegar, 2 tablespoons soy sauce, sugar, 2 teaspoons cornflour, and chilli paste; set aside.

(See stir-frying photos, pages 24–25.) Preheat a wok or large frying pan over high heat; add *1 tablespoon* of the cooking oil. Stir-fry garlic in hot oil for 15 seconds. Add spring onions; stir-fry about 1½ minutes or until crisp-tender. Remove onions (see photo 1, page 31).

Add remaining cooking oil to the hot wok or frying pan. (Add more cooking oil as necessary during cooking.) Add chicken (see photo 2, page 31). Stir-fry about 3 minutes or until done. Push from the centre of the wok.

Stir sauce; add to the centre of the wok or frying pan. Cook and stir until thickened and bubbly. Return onions to the wok; add water chestnuts and bamboo shoots. Stir ingredients together to coat with sauce (see photo 3, page 31). Cook and stir for 1 minute more. Stir in peanuts and sesame oil, if desired. Makes 4 servings.

See cutting technique, page 27.

Pork with Fish Flavour

The sweet and spicy sauce in this dish does not contain fish. Rather, it is made with the same ingredients often used by Szechwan cooks to cook fish—hence the name.

1 pound (450g) boneless pork
2 tablespoons rice wine *or* dry sherry
1 tablespoon soy sauce
6 dried wood ears
5 spring onions
2 cloves garlic
Root ginger
2 fluid ounces (55ml) water
3 tablespoons soy sauce
2 teaspoons caster sugar
2 teaspoons cornflour
1 teaspoon rice vinegar *or* vinegar
¼ teaspoon whole Szechwan peppers *or* whole black peppers, crushed
1 tablespoon cooking oil
1 teaspoon Oriental chilli paste
8 ounces (225g) tinned sliced water chestnuts, drained

Partially freeze pork; bias-slice across the grain into strips. Cut strips into matchstick-size shreds (see tip, page 35). For marinade, in a medium mixing bowl combine *1 tablespoon* of the rice wine or dry sherry and 1 tablespoon soy sauce; stir in pork. Cover and let stand at room temperature for 30 minutes, stirring occasionally. (*Or,* marinate in the refrigerator for 2 hours.)

Meanwhile, in a small mixing bowl soak wood ears in enough hot water to cover for 30 minutes. Rinse well and squeeze to drain thoroughly. Slice thinly, discarding stems; set aside.

Bias-slice spring onions into 1-inch (2.5cm) pieces.* Mince garlic.* Grate 2 teaspoons root ginger.* For sauce, in a small mixing bowl stir together remaining rice wine or dry sherry, water, 3 tablespoons soy sauce, sugar, cornflour, rice vinegar or vinegar, and crushed Szechwan or black pepper; set aside.

(See stir-frying photos, pages 24–25.) Preheat a wok or large frying pan over high heat; add oil. (Add more oil as necessary during cooking.) Stir-fry garlic, root ginger, and chilli paste in hot oil for 15 seconds. Add wood ears and spring onions; stir-fry about 1½ minutes or until spring onions are crisp-tender. Remove spring onion mixture (see photo 1, page 31).

Add *half* of the pork to the hot wok or frying pan (see photo 2, page 31). Stir-fry for 2 to 3 minutes or until no pink remains. Remove pork. Stir-fry remaining pork for 2 to 3 minutes or until no pink remains. Return all pork to the wok. Push from the centre of the wok.

Stir sauce; add to the centre of the wok or frying pan. Cook and stir until thickened and bubbly. Return spring onion mixture to the wok; add water chestnuts. Stir ingredients together to coat with sauce (see photo 3, page 31). Cook and stir for 1 minute more. Makes 4 servings.

Szechwan-Style Pork and Cabbage

12 ounces (350g) boneless pork
½ of a medium head Chinese cabbage
4 spring onions
1 medium green pepper
1 clove garlic
Root ginger
1 tablespoon soy sauce
2 teaspoons cornflour
1 to 2 teaspoons Oriental chilli sauce or
½ teaspoon ground red pepper
1 tablespoon cooking oil

Partially freeze pork; bias-slice across the grain into bite-size strips (see tip, opposite). Chop cabbage into 1-inch (2.5cm) pieces. Bias-slice spring onions into 1-inch (2.5cm) pieces.* Cut green pepper into strips. Mince garlic.* Grate 1 teaspoon root ginger.* For sauce, mix soy sauce, cornflour, chilli sauce or red pepper, and 4 fluid ounces (110ml) *water;* set aside.

(See stir-frying photos, pages 24–25.) Preheat a wok or large frying pan over high heat; add oil. (Add more oil as necessary during cooking.) Stir-fry garlic and root ginger in hot oil for 15 seconds. Add spring onions and green pepper; stir-fry for 1½ to 2 minutes or until crisp-tender. Remove onion mixture (see photo 1, page 31).

Add pork to hot wok or frying pan (see photo 2, page 31). Stir-fry for 3 to 4 minutes or until no pink remains. Push from centre of the wok.

Stir sauce; add to centre of wok or frying pan. Cook and stir until thickened and bubbly. Return onion mixture to wok; add cabbage. Stir to coat with sauce (see photo 3, page 31). Cook and stir 1 minute more. Makes 4 servings.

Boning Chicken Breasts

Skinning
Place the whole chicken breast on a cutting board, skin side up. Starting on one side of the breast, pull the skin away from the meat, using your hand, as shown. Discard the skin.

Boning
Cut the meat away from one side of the breastbone, using a thin sharp knife. Then, move the knife over the rib bones, pulling away the meat, as shown. Repeat on the other side.

Removing Tendon
For each breast half, hold one end of the long white tendon with your fingers. Use the tip of the knife to scrape the meat away from the tendon as you pull it out of the breast meat, as shown.

*See cutting technique, page 27.

Peking Lamb With Spring Onions

Create a rich flavour blend with two types of soy sauce.

1 pound (450g) boneless lamb
1 tablespoon rice wine *or* dry sherry
1 tablespoon light soy sauce
10 spring onions
2 cloves garlic
1 tablespoon rice wine *or* dry sherry
1 tablespoon dark soy sauce
½ teaspoon caster sugar
½ teaspoon sesame oil (optional)
1 tablespoon cooking oil

Partially freeze lamb; bias-slice across the grain into bite-size strips (*see tip, below*). For marinade, in a medium mixing bowl mix 1 tablespoon rice wine or dry sherry and light soy sauce; stir in lamb. Cover and let stand at room temperature for 30 minutes, stirring occasionally. (*Or,* marinate in the refrigerator for 2 hours.)

Sliver spring onions.* Mince garlic.* For sauce, mix 1 tablespoon rice wine or dry sherry, dark soy sauce, sugar, and sesame oil, if desired.

(See stir-frying photos, pages 24–25.) Preheat a wok or large frying pan over high heat; add cooking oil. (Add more oil as necessary during cooking.) Stir-fry garlic in hot oil for 15 seconds. Add onions; stir-fry for 1½ minutes or until crisp-tender. Remove onions (*see photo 1, page 31*). Add *half* of the lamb to the hot wok (*see photo 2, page 31*). Stir-fry for 2 to 3 minutes or until done. Remove lamb. Stir-fry remaining lamb for 2 to 3 minutes or until done. Return all lamb to the wok. Push from the centre of the wok. Stir sauce; add to the centre of the wok. Cook and stir about 30 seconds or until heated through. Return onions to the wok; stir together to coat with sauce (*see photo 3, page 31*). Cook and stir for 1 minute more. Makes 4 servings.

Cutting Meat and Poultry

Bias Slicing
Partially freeze the meat about 20 minutes for easier cutting. Then, with a sharp knife or a cleaver, thinly slice the meat at a 45-degree angle. Cook at once or return to refrigerator.

Shredding
Bias-slice the meat (*see photo, left*). Then, stack two or three slices of meat together and cut the slices lengthwise into matchstick-size shreds, as shown.

Cubing
Remove skin, bones, and tendon from each chicken breast half (*see tip, opposite*). Cut meat lengthwise into 1-inch (2.5cm)-wide strips. Then, cut strips crosswise into cubes, as shown.

Stir-Fried Rice

Thanks to the ingenuity of Oriental cooks, we have fried rice. Though it relies on leftovers, fried rice is one of the tastiest stir-frys ever created.

Bits of meat or seafood and vegetables, seasonings, and cold boiled rice are transformed into beautiful stir-fried masterpieces. Wherever you go in the Orient, you'll find fried rice dishes as varied as the cooks who make them. Here is a sampling of our favourite fried rice recipes.

Yangchow Fried Rice

Yangchow Fried Rice

Fried rice is typically prepared with ham in eastern China; roast pork is used in the southern region.

20 **ounces (560g) Chinese Boiled Rice (see recipe, right)**
 4 **ounces (110g) fresh or frozen shelled prawns (see tip, page 21)**
 4 **ounces (110g) fully cooked ham *or* Chinese Roast Pork (see recipe, page 10)**
7½ **ounces (210g) tinned straw mushrooms**
 2 **medium Webb lettuce leaves**
 1 **spring onion**
 2 **tablespoons cooking oil**
 2 **beaten eggs**
 2 **ounces (50g) frozen peas, thawed**
 2 **tablespoons chicken broth *or* dark soy sauce**

Prepare Chinese Boiled Rice; chill thoroughly. In a small saucepan bring 16 fluid ounces (425ml) *water* and ¼ teaspoon *salt* to the boil; add prawns. Return to the boil; reduce heat and simmer, uncovered, for 1 to 3 minutes or until prawns turn pink, stirring occasionally. Rinse and drain. Chop prawns.

Finely dice ham or Chinese Roast Pork. Drain mushrooms and chop. Finely shred Webb lettuce leaves. Thinly slice spring onion.

Preheat a wok or large frying pan over medium heat; add *1 tablespoon* of oil. Add eggs; lift and tilt wok to form a thin "egg sheet" (see photo 3). Cook, without stirring, about 2 minutes or just until set. Slide egg sheet onto cutting board. Cut into ¾-inch (2cm) -wide strips (see photo 4). Cut strips into 2-inch (5cm) lengths.

(See stir-frying photos, pages 24–25 and 30–31.) Return the wok or frying pan to high heat. Add remaining oil to the hot wok. (Add more oil as necessary during cooking.) Stir-fry prawns, ham or pork, mushrooms, and peas in hot oil for 1 minute. Add rice, spring onion, and chicken broth or soy sauce; stir for 1 minute or until heated through. Stir in egg strips. Cover and cook for 1 minute. Add Webb; toss lightly. Makes 6 side-dish servings.

Chinese Boiled Rice

 8 **ounces (200g) long grain rice**
16 **fluid ounces (425ml) cold water**
 ¼ **teaspoon salt**

If using imported rice, wash uncooked rice under cold running water, rubbing grains together with fingers, until water runs clear (see photo 1). Drain well.

In a medium saucepan combine rice, 16 fluid ounces (425ml) cold water, and salt. Bring to the boil; reduce heat to low and cover with a tight-fitting lid. Simmer for 20 minutes or until small pockets form on the surface of the rice (see photo 2). Remove from heat. Let stand, covered, for 10 minutes. Fluff rice with a fork. Makes 20 ounces (560g).

1 If you use rice imported from an Asian country, wash it in a sieve under cold running water till the water runs clear.

2 The rice is done when small pockets appear on the surface of the rice. If the pockets contain water, cover the saucepan and continue cooking till the water is absorbed by the rice.

3 Lift and tilt the wok or frying pan to form a thin layer of egg, known as an egg sheet. Work quickly because the egg begins to set as soon as it touches the hot wok or frying pan.

4 Slide the egg sheet from the wok onto a cutting board. Using a sharp knife, cut the egg into ¾-inch (2cm) -wide strips, as shown. Then, cut the narrow egg strips into 2-inch (5cm) lengths.

Nasi Goreng

Garnishes play an important part in Nasi Goreng in Indonesia and Malaysia.

20   **ounces (560g) Chinese Boiled Rice
       (see recipe, page 38)**
 8   **ounces (225g) boneless pork or beef
       rumpsteak**
 4   **ounces (110g) fresh *or* frozen shelled
       prawns (see tip, page 21)**
 6   **spring onions**
 1   **small cucumber**
 1   **medium onion**
 2   **cloves garlic**
 1   **teaspoon shrimp paste *or* anchovy
       paste**
 ½   **teaspoon crushed red pepper *or*
       ¼ teaspoon ground red pepper**
 2   **tablespoons water**
 2   **tablespoons cooking oil**
 2   **beaten eggs**
 2   **tablespoons soy sauce**

Prepare Chinese Boiled Rice; chill thoroughly. Partially freeze pork or beef; bias-slice across the grain into bite-size strips (see tip, page 35). Thaw prawns, if frozen; rinse and pat dry. Halve prawns lengthwise. (If prawn are large, halve again crosswise.) Set aside.

Bias-slice spring onions into 1-inch (2.5cm) pieces.* Thinly slice unpeeled cucumber. Thinly slice onion. Mince garlic.* In a small mixing bowl combine garlic, shrimp paste or anchovy paste, and crushed red pepper or ground red pepper; gradually stir in water. Add to pork or beef, tossing to coat; set aside.

Preheat a wok or large frying pan over medium heat; add *1 tablespoon* of the oil. Add eggs; lift and tilt the wok or frying pan to form a thin "egg sheet" (see photo 3, page 39). Cook, without stirring, about 2 minutes or just until set. Slide egg sheet onto a cutting board. Cut into ¾-inch (2cm)-wide strips (see photo 4, page 39). Cut strips into 2-inch (5cm) lengths.

(See stir-frying photos, pages 24–25 and 30–31.) Return the wok or frying pan to high heat. Add remaining oil to the hot wok. (Add more oil as necessary during cooking.) Stir-fry thinly sliced onion in hot oil for 1½ to 2 minutes or until golden brown; remove onion. Add pork or beef mixture; stir-fry for 2 minutes. Add prawns and spring onions; stir-fry for 1½ to 2 minutes or until meat and prawns are done.

Add rice and soy sauce; stir for 1 minute or until heated through. Stir in *half* of the egg strips. Cover and cook for 1 minute. To serve, spoon fried rice onto a serving dish. Garnish with browned onion slices, remaining egg strips, and cucumber. Makes 4 servings.

Nuoc Cham

Vietnamese cooks serve a tangy hot sauce, Nuoc Cham, as a table or dipping sauce at most meals. Chill any unused sauce.

3   **tablespoons caster sugar**
2   **red *or* green chilli peppers, seeded and
      finely chopped (see Note, page 30)**
4   **cloves garlic, minced***
3   **fluid ounces (80ml) lime juice**
2   **tablespoons vinegar**
2   **tablespoons fish sauce**
2   **teaspoons water**

In a small mixing bowl combine sugar, chilli peppers, and garlic. Stir in lime juice, vinegar, fish sauce, and water. Makes about 5 fluid ounces (140ml).

See cutting technique, page 27.

Fried Rice with Sausage and Crab

When you can't buy sweet and pungent flavoured Chinese sausage, try using salami.

20 **ounces (560g) Chinese Boiled Rice (see recipe, page 38)**
4 **dried mushrooms**
 Nuoc Cham (optional) (see recipe, opposite)
2 **Chinese sausage links**
6 **ounces (175g) tinned crabmeat**
6 **spring onions**
2 **tablespoons cooking oil**
2 **beaten eggs**
1 **tablespoon fish sauce**

Prepare Chinese Boiled Rice; chill thoroughly. In a small mixing bowl soak mushrooms in enough hot water to cover for 30 minutes. Rinse well; squeeze to drain thoroughly. Thinly slice mushrooms, discarding stems; set aside.

Meanwhile, prepare Nuoc Cham, if desired. Thinly slice sausage links. Drain crabmeat and remove cartilage, if present. Flake crabmeat. Thinly slice spring onions.

Preheat a wok or large frying pan over medium heat; add *1 tablespoon* of the oil. Add eggs; lift and tilt the wok or frying pan to form a thin "egg sheet" (see photo 3, page 39). Cook, without stirring, about 2 minutes or just until set. Slide egg sheet onto a cutting board. Cut into ¾-inch (2cm)-wide strips (see photo 4, page 39). Cut strips into 2-inch (5cm) lengths.

(See stir-frying photos, pages 24–25 and 30–31.) Return the wok or frying pan to high heat. Add remaining oil to the hot wok. (Add more oil as necessary during cooking.) Stir-fry sausages and mushrooms in hot oil about 2 minutes or until sausage is light brown.

Add rice, crabmeat, spring onions, and fish sauce; stir for 1 minute or until heated through. Stir in egg strips. Cover and cook for 1 minute. Serve with Nuoc Cham, if desired. Serves 4.

Fried Rice With Chicken

If you don't have shrimp powder for this Thai-flavoured rice dish, grind a few dried shrimp in the blender.

20 **ounces (560g) Chinese Boiled Rice (see recipe, page 38)**
1 **whole medium chicken breast (about 12 ounces [350g]), skinned and boned (see tip, page 34)**
8 **ounces (225g) tofu (fresh bean curd)**
1 **medium onion**
2 **cloves garlic**
 Fresh cilantro *or* parsley
2 **tablespoons fish sauce**
1 **to 2 teaspoons Oriental chilli sauce *or* ½ teaspoon ground red pepper**
½ **teaspoon shrimp powder *or* 1 teaspoon shrimp paste**
2 **tablespoons cooking oil**
2 **beaten eggs**
1 **tablespoon lime juice**

Prepare Chinese Boiled Rice; chill thoroughly. Cut chicken into thin bite-size strips. Drain tofu; cut into ½-inch (1cm) cubes. Chop onion. Mince garlic.* Snip 2 tablespoons cilantro or parsley. In a mixing bowl mix fish sauce, chilli sauce or red pepper, and shrimp powder or shrimp paste.

Preheat a wok or large frying pan over medium heat; add *1 tablespoon* of the oil. Add eggs; lift and tilt the wok or frying pan to form a thin "egg sheet" (see photo 3, page 39). Cook, without stirring, about 2 minutes or just until set. Slide egg sheet onto a cutting board. Cut into ¾-inch (2cm)-wide strips (see photo 4, page 39). Cut strips into 2-inch (5cm) lengths.

(See stir-frying photos, pages 24–25 and 30–31.) Return the wok or frying pan to high heat. Add remaining oil to the hot wok. (Add more oil as necessary during cooking.) Stir-fry onion and garlic for 1½ minutes. Add chicken; stir-fry for 2 to 3 minutes or until chicken is done. Add rice and fish sauce mixture; stir for 1 minute or until heated through. Gently stir in tofu and egg strips. Cover and cook for 1 minute. Add cilantro or parsley and lime juice; toss lightly. Makes 4 servings.

42

Pan-Fried Noodles

Egg noodles—crisp and golden brown on the outside, yet tender and moist on the inside. Sound too good to be true? Pan-fry Chinese egg noodles and taste for yourself.

Thought to be a forerunner of deep-fried chow-mein noodles, pan-fried noodles are shaped into a noodle cake and browned. Serve the noodle cake topped with any of our delicious stir-frys.

Stir-Fried Chicken with Noodle Cake

Stir-Fried Chicken With Noodle Cake

2 **whole large chicken breasts (about 2 pounds [900g] total), skinned and boned (see tip, page 34)**
3 **tablespoons rice wine *or* dry sherry**
3 **tablespoons soy sauce**
1 **teaspoon sesame oil (optional)**
½ **of a medium head bok choy**
2 **medium carrots**
6 **ounces (175g) fresh mange tout *or* frozen mange tout, thawed**
2 **cloves garlic**
  Root ginger
10 **fluid ounces (275ml) chicken broth**
2 **tablespoons cornflour**
  Pan-Fried Noodle Cake (see recipe, right)
1 **tablespoon cooking oil**

Cut chicken into thin bite-size strips. For marinade, in a medium mixing bowl combine *1 tablespoon* of the rice wine or dry sherry; *1 tablespoon* of the soy sauce; and sesame oil, if desired. Stir in chicken. Cover and let stand at room temperature for 30 minutes, stirring occasionally. (*Or,* marinate chicken in the refrigerator for 2 hours.)

Chop bok choy.* Cut carrots into julienne strips.* If using fresh mange tout, remove tips and strings. Mince garlic.* Grate 1 tablespoon root ginger.* For sauce, in a small mixing bowl combine chicken broth, cornflour, remaining rice wine or dry sherry, and remaining soy sauce; set aside.

Prepare Pan-Fried Noodle Cake; keep warm. Drain chicken, reserving marinade. Add marinade to sauce mixture; set aside.

(See stir-frying photos, pages 24–25 and 30–31.) Preheat a wok or large frying pan over high heat; add cooking oil. (Add more oil as necessary during cooking.) Stir-fry garlic and root ginger in hot oil for 15 seconds. Add carrots; stir-fry for 1 minute. Add bok choy; stir-fry for 1 minute. Add mange tout; stir-fry for 2 minutes

See cutting technique, page 27.

or until crisp-tender. Remove vegetables. Add *half* of the chicken to the hot wok or frying pan. Stir-fry for 2 to 3 minutes or until done. Remove chicken. Stir-fry remaining chicken for 2 to 3 minutes or until done. Return all chicken to the wok. Push from the centre of the wok.

Stir sauce; add to the centre of the wok or frying pan. Cook and stir until thickened and bubbly. Return vegetables to the wok; stir to coat with sauce. Cook and stir for 1 minute more.

To serve, slide noodle cake onto a serving dish. Spoon some chicken stir-fry over noodles (see photo 4). Pass remaining stir-fry. Serves 6.

Pan-Fried Noodle Cake

8 **ounces (225g) fresh *or* dried Chinese egg noodles *or* fine egg noodles**
1 **tablespoon cooking oil**

In a large covered casserole bring 4¾ pints (2.7l) *water* and 1 tablespoon *salt* to the boil. Add noodles; cook till tender, stirring occasionally. Allow 4 minutes for fresh Chinese noodles, 6 minutes for dried Chinese noodles, 2 minutes for fresh egg noodles, and 4 minutes for dried egg noodles. Drain and rinse with cold water. Drain well.

In a heavy 10-inch (25.5cm) ovenproof frying pan with nonstick coating, heat oil over medium heat. Pat noodles in the frying pan (see photo 1). Cook, uncovered, for 5 to 6 minutes or till the bottoms of the noodles are light brown. Loosen noodles around the edge, then invert the frying pan and noodles onto a large plate (see photo 2).

Slide noodle cake back into the frying pan, brown side up (see photo 3). Cook, uncovered, for 5 to 6 minutes more or till the bottom is light brown. Remove from heat; keep warm in a 300°F (150°C) gas mark 2 oven while preparing stir-fry. Makes 6 servings.

1 Using the backside of a wooden spoon, gently pat the well-drained noodles in the frying pan, making the top of the noodles as smooth as possible.

2 Invert a large plate over the frying pan. Holding them together, invert the frying pan onto the plate to remove the noodle cake. Then, lift off the frying pan, as shown.

3 To brown the other side of the noodle cake, slide the noodles, brown side up, from the plate into the frying pan, pushing gently with a wooden spoon.

4 Spoon the stir-fry mixture over the noodle cake. Then, cut the cake into wedges.

Roast Pork with Crispy Noodles

Finely chop the leftover roast pork and sprinkle it over creamy soups or vegetable soups.

 1 **pound (450g) Chinese Roast Pork (see recipe, page 10)**
 2 **small courgettes**
 4 **ounces tinned water chestnuts, sliced**
    Root ginger
12 **fluid ounces (330ml) chicken broth**
 3 **tablespoons cornflour**
 2 **to 3 tablespoons oyster sauce**
    Pan-Fried Noodle Cake (see recipe, page 44)
 1 **tablespoon cooking oil**

Prepare Chinese Roast Pork, *except* omit serving suggestion. Cut pork into thin bite-size strips. Cut courgettes into julienne strips.* Drain water chestnuts. Grate 2 teaspoons root ginger.* For sauce, in a mixing bowl mix chicken broth, cornflour, and oyster sauce; set aside. Prepare Pan-Fried Noodle Cake; keep warm.

(See stir-frying photos, pages 24–25 and 30–31.) Preheat a wok or large frying pan over high heat; add oil. (Add more oil as necessary during cooking.) Stir-fry root ginger in hot oil for 15 seconds. Add courgettes; stir-fry for 2 to 3 minutes or until crisp-tender. Remove courgettes.

Add pork to the hot wok or frying pan; stir-fry for 2 to 3 minutes or until heated through. Push from the centre of the wok.

Stir sauce; add to the centre of the wok or frying pan. Cook and stir until thickened and bubbly. Return courgettes to the wok; add water chestnuts. Stir ingredients together to coat with sauce. Cook and stir for 1 minute more.

To serve, slide noodle cake onto a serving dish. Spoon pork stir-fry over noodles (see photo 4, page 45). Makes 6 servings.

Beef and Tomatoes With Fried Noodles

 1 **pound (450g) chuck *or* blade bone steak**
 1 **medium green pepper**
 4 **spring onions**
 2 **medium tomatoes**
 2 **cloves garlic**
 6 **fluid ounces (165ml) chicken broth**
 2 **tablespoons cornflour**
 2 **tablespoons soy sauce**
 1 **tablespoon rice vinegar *or* vinegar**
 1 **tablespoon dry sherry**
 1 **teaspoon caster sugar**
½ **to 1 teaspoon Oriental chilli paste**
    Pan-Fried Noodle Cake (see recipe, page 44)
 1 **tablespoon cooking oil**

Partially freeze beef; bias-slice across the grain into bite-size strips (see tip, page 35). Cut green pepper into julienne strips.* Bias-slice spring onions into ½-inch (1cm) pieces.* Cut tomatoes into wedges. Mince garlic.* For sauce, in a small mixing bowl combine chicken broth, cornflour, soy sauce, rice vinegar or vinegar, dry sherry, sugar, and chilli paste; set aside. Prepare Pan-Fried Noodle Cake; keep warm.

(See stir-frying photos, pages 24–25 and 30–31.) Preheat a wok or large frying pan over high heat; add oil. (Add more oil as necessary during cooking.) Stir-fry garlic in hot oil for 15 seconds. Add green pepper and spring onion; stir-fry about 1½ minutes or until vegetables are crisp-tender. Remove onion mixture.

Add *half* of the beef to the hot wok or frying pan. Stir-fry for 2 to 3 minutes or until done. Remove beef. Stir-fry remaining beef for 2 to 3 minutes or until done. Return all beef to the wok. Push from the centre of the wok.

Stir sauce; add to the centre of the wok or frying pan. Cook and stir until thickened and bubbly. Return onion mixture to the wok; add tomatoes. Stir together to coat with sauce. Cover and cook for 1 minute more. To serve, slide noodle cake onto a serving dish. Spoon beef stir-fry over noodles (see photo 4, page 45). Serves 6.

See cutting technique, page 27.

Cuisines at a Glance

The style and flavour of each Oriental country's cuisine reflect its resources as well as the influences of neighbouring lands.

Chinese

Chinese food is commonly divided into regional styles of cooking. Although alike in many respects, each area is unique.

Northern cuisine (Peking or Mandarin) has wheat as its staple grain. It appears in noodles, pancakes, and buns. Other common ingredients in the diet include lamb, tofu, spring onions, soy sauce, and garlic.

Eastern cuisine (Shanghai) focuses on the seaport city of Shanghai. Fish and seafood are available, as well as agricultural crops from inland areas. Seasonings are often delicate but slightly sweet. Red-cooking is a specialty.

Southern cuisine (Cantonese) centres on the seaport city of Canton. Known for their stir-frys and dim sum, Cantonese cooks pride themselves on preserving the natural flavour of food, using mildly seasoned sauces.

Western cuisine (Szechwan) is found inland and includes the provinces of Szechwan and Hunan. Highly seasoned and spicy hot, this cuisine makes use of hot chilli peppers, spring onions, root ginger, vinegar, Szechwan peppers, garlic, dried mushrooms, and dried tangerine peel.

Japanese

The artistic presentation of food is of great importance in Japan. Japanese cooks insist on freshness in their food and prefer delicate seasonings. They stress seasonal foods prepared in a simple manner. Tofu and short grain rice are staples in their diet.

Korean

Korean food has similarities to both Chinese and Japanese cuisines, yet it has a boldness of its own. Beef is popular, as are pork and chicken. Basic seasonings are garlic, spring onions, soy sauce, root ginger, ground pepper, sesame seed, and sesame oil. Rice appears daily, along with pickled vegetables.

Vietnamese

The food of Vietnam reflects the influences of China, India, France, and all of Southeast Asia. Seafood, fresh fruits, and raw vegetables are used extensively. Fish sauce is a universal seasoning both in cooking and at the table. Coconut milk sweetens many dishes.

Thai

Thailand's cooking differs from that of its neighbours in that Thai cooks do not thicken their sauces. Favourite seasonings include chilli peppers, fish sauce, shrimp paste, coconut, coriander (cilantro), garlic, and citrus flavourings (lemongrass and citrus leaves).

Indonesian and Malaysian

Closely related, these cuisines combine spices, chilli peppers, shrimp paste, and coconuts to achieve unusual flavour blends. Although not all foods are hot and spicy, their flavour is seldom subtle.

Bubbling Hot Pots

Let your guests share in
the fun of cooking: Serve
an Oriental hot pot.
Everyone joins in, selecting
and cooking the food in a
pot of simmering broth.
Japanese cooks use
an earthenware casserole
called a *do nabé* (doh
NAH bay), and the
Chinese cook in a heavy
metal Mongolian firepot.
An electric wok or an
electric frying pan makes
an ideal substitute.

Chicken and Vegetable One-Pot

Chicken and Vegetable One-Pot

Oriental chrysanthemum leaves add fragrance to Japanese one-pots. Not to be confused with the toxic common flowering plant, shungiku is sold in Oriental markets or can be grown from seed at home.

3 **whole medium chicken breasts (about 2¼ pounds [1kg10g] total), skinned and boned (see tip, page 34)**
1 **4-inch (10cm) piece (1 ounce [25g]) fresh burdock root (gobo)**
24 **fluid ounces (680ml) Dashi (see recipe, page 20)**
4 **ounces (110g) Oriental chrysanthemum leaves *or* torn fresh spinach**
4 **ounces (110g) fresh *or* dried udon (thick white noodles)**
3 **ounces (75g) enoki mushrooms, root ends removed**
2 **leeks, thinly bias sliced***
8 **ounces (225g) tofu (fresh bean curd), cut into ½-inch (1cm) cubes**
3 **fluid ounces (80ml) light soy sauce**
2 **tablespoons mirin**
1 **tablespoon caster sugar**

Thinly slice chicken into bite-size strips; set aside. Trim burdock; wash and scrub. Cut into thin shavings (see photo 1). Soak in cold water for 10 minutes; drain. Prepare Dashi.

Rinse chrysanthemum leaves or spinach; drain. If using chrysanthemum leaves, discard roots and flowering buds, if present.

In a large covered casserole bring 64 fluid ounces (1.8l) *water* and 1 teaspoon *salt* to boiling. Snip or break udon into 3- to 4-inch (7.5 to 10cm) lengths. Add to boiling water; cook about 10 minutes or until nearly tender, stirring occasionally. Drain; rinse with cold water. Drain well. Place in a zaru (Japanese bamboo draining basket) or a serving bowl.

Meanwhile, arrange chicken, burdock, chrysanthemum leaves or spinach, enoki, leeks, and tofu on a serving dish (see photo 2).

See cutting technique, page 27.

About 10 minutes before serving, in a do nabé placed over a tableside heating unit, electric frying pan, or electric wok, combine Dashi, soy sauce, mirin, and sugar. Bring to boiling, stirring until sugar dissolves. Reduce heat to simmering. Add *half* of each of the chicken, burdock, enoki, leeks, and tofu; simmer for 4 minutes. Add *half* of the chrysanthemum leaves or spinach; simmer for 1 minute.

Let all use chopsticks to help themselves (see tip, below). Repeat, cooking remaining chicken, vegetables, tofu, and greens.

Add udon to broth. Cook about 1½ minutes or until heated through. Ladle into soup bowls (see photo 3). Serve as soup. Makes 6 servings.

Using Chopsticks: Place one chopstick, about two-thirds of its length from the narrow tip, in the curve at the base of your thumb. Let the stick rest on the end of your ring finger. Close the base of your thumb over the stick to hold it firm. This stick does not move.

Now hold the second chopstick firmly between the tip of your thumb and your index finger, with the middle finger resting on the first stick.

To pick up food, use your index finger to move the top stick up and down, bringing the tip in contact with the tip of the stationary stick.

3 When all of the meat or seafood and vegetables have been eaten, ladle the full-flavoured broth into soup bowls, as shown.

1 Using a sharp knife, cut the burdock into thin shavings, as if sharpening a pencil. Immediately soak the shavings in cold water so they won't discolour.

2 Arrange the food on one or more serving dishes. To reduce last-minute tasks, clean and cut the food earlier in the day, then cover and chill till serving time.

Mongolian Firepot

1½ pounds (700g) boneless lamb
½ of a medium head Chinese cabbage, sliced about ½ inch (1cm) thick
2 ounces (50g) bean threads
 Sesame Paste Dip (see recipe, right)
4 ounces (110g) dried buckwheat noodles *or* dried fine egg noodles
64 fluid ounces (1.8l) chicken broth *or* water
4 spring onions, cut into 1½-inch (4cm) slivers
2 tablespoons grated root ginger

Partially freeze lamb; bias-slice across the grain into bite-size strips (see tip, page 35). Arrange lamb and cabbage on a serving dish (see photo 2, page 51).

In a large mixing bowl soak bean threads in enough hot water to cover for 30 minutes. Drain well. Cut into 3- to 4-inch (7.5 to 10cm) lengths (see photo 1, page 18). Place in a serving bowl. Prepare Sesame Paste Dip; set aside.

In a large covered casserole bring 64 fluid ounces (1.8l) *water* and 1 teaspoon *salt* to the boil. Break noodles into 3- to 4-inch (7.5 to 10cm) lengths. Add to boiling water; cook until nearly tender, stirring occasionally. Allow about 10 minutes for buckwheat noodles and 4 minutes for egg noodles. Drain; rinse with cold water. Drain well. Place in a serving bowl.

If using a firepot,** about 30 minutes before serving, line a heatproof pan with heavy foil. Outdoors, pile briquettes into a pyramid on the foil, then light (see tip, opposite). (The coals are ready to use when they appear ash grey.)

In a large saucepan bring broth or water to the boil; add spring onions and root ginger. Pour into the firepot or electric wok or frying pan until *half* full. Keep remaining broth warm; replenish pot as necessary. If using a firepot, cover the pot. Lower coals down the firepot chimney, resting them on the grate. Remove cover.

To serve, give each person a small bowl of dip and a wire strainer or chopsticks (see tip, page 50). Dip lamb into simmering broth for 30 to 60 seconds or until done. Remove and eat with dip.

After half of the lamb has been cooked, let each person add some of the bean threads, noodles, or cabbage to broth. Cook bean threads and noodles about 1½ minutes or until heated through. Cook cabbage about 2 minutes or until crisp-tender. Remove from broth; eat with dip, if desired. Repeat, cooking remaining food.

Ladle remaining broth into soup bowls (see photo 3, page 51). Let each person season broth with remaining dip, if desired. Serves 6.

**Note: If a firepot is unavailable, use an electric wok or an electric frying pan. Omit directions for using briquettes.

Sesame Paste Dip

Freeze leftover dip to use another time.

1 ounce (25g) sesame paste, Sesame Paste (see tip, page 11), *or* peanut butter
2 tablespoons fermented bean curd (red), drained; fermented bean curd with chilli, drained; *or* sweet red bean paste
2 tablespoons soy sauce
1 tablespoon sesame oil *or* cooking oil
1 tablespoon chilli oil *or* Chilli Oil (see Note, page 11)
1 to 2 teaspoons Oriental chilli sauce *or* ½ teaspoon ground red pepper

In a food processor bowl or a blender place all ingredients and 2 fluid ounces (55ml) *water*. Cover; process or blend until smooth. Makes about 8 fluid ounces (220ml).

*See cutting technique, page 27.

Cantonese Firepot

8 ounces (225g) beef sirloin
1 whole medium chicken breast (about
   12 ounces [350g]), skinned and
   boned (see tip, page 34)
8 ounces (225g) fresh *or* frozen prawns
   in shells
4 ounces (110g) fresh *or* frozen scallops
   Soy-Vinegar Sauce
   Hot Mustard Sauce (see recipe,
   page 10)
4 ounces (110g) fresh or dried Chinese
   egg noodles or fine egg noodles
4 ounces (110g) tofu (fresh bean curd),
   cut into ½-inch (1cm) cubes
9 ounces (250g) sliced bok choy
4 ounces (110g) sliced lettuce
8 ounces (225g) torn fresh spinach
3 ounces (75g) torn watercress
64 fluid ounces (1.8l) chicken broth

Partially freeze beef; bias-slice across the grain into bite-size strips (see tip, page 35). Thinly slice chicken into bite-size strips. Thaw prawns and scallops, if frozen. Shell and devein prawns (see tip, page 21). Halve prawns lengthwise. Halve large scallops. Arrange beef, chicken, prawns, and scallops on a serving dish (see photo 2, page 51). Prepare sauces; set aside.

Bring 64 fluid ounces (1.8l) *water* and 1 teaspoon *salt* to the boil. Snip or break noodles into 3- to 4-inch (7.5 to 10cm) lengths. Add to boiling water; cook until nearly tender, stirring occasionally. Allow 4 minutes for fresh Chinese noodles, 6 minutes for dried Chinese noodles, 2 minutes for fresh egg noodles, and 4 minutes for dried egg noodles. Drain; rinse with cold water. Drain well. Place in a serving bowl. Arrange tofu and greens on a serving dish.

If using a firepot,** about 30 minutes before serving, line a heatproof pan with heavy foil. Outdoors, pile briquettes into a pyramid on the foil, then light (see tip, right). (The coals are ready when they appear ash grey.) In a large saucepan bring broth to the boil. Pour into the firepot, electric wok, or electric frying pan until *half* full. Keep remaining broth warm; replenish

the pot as necessary. If using a firepot, cover the pot. Lower coals down firepot chimney, resting them on the grate. Remove cover.

To serve, give each person a small bowl of *each* sauce and a small wire strainer or chopsticks (see tip, page 50). Dip meat or seafood into simmering broth until done. Allow 30 to 60 seconds for beef, 1 to 2 minutes for chicken, and 2½ to 3 minutes for seafood. Remove from broth; eat with sauces. After half of the meat and seafood has been cooked, let each person add some of the tofu or greens to broth. Cook tofu, lettuce, spinach, and watercress about 1½ minutes or until heated through. Cook bok choy about 3 minutes or until crisp-tender. Remove from broth; eat with sauces. Repeat, cooking remaining meat, seafood, tofu, and greens. Add noodles to broth. Cook for 1½ minutes or until heated through. Ladle into soup bowls (see photo 3, page 51). Makes 6 servings.

Soy-Vinegar Sauce: Mix 3 fluid ounces (80ml) *soy sauce,* 3 fluid ounces (80ml) *Chinese black vinegar or rice vinegar,* and 1 *spring onion,* thinly sliced. Makes 5 fluid ounces (140ml).

Note: If a firepot is unavailable, use an electric wok or an electric frying pan. Omit directions for using briquettes.

Firepot Safety

● Always use a firepot outdoors because the coals produce toxic gases as they burn.
● To prevent damage to the pot, lower the coals down the firepot chimney onto the grate *after* adding the hot broth to the pot.
● Add more coals every 20 to 30 minutes, if needed.

Delectable Egg Dumplings

Petite and omelette-shaped, these egg dumplings burst with a savoury filling. In China, the bright yellow colour of the dumplings is likened to gold coins. According to Chinese lore, serving these tender morsels conveys a wish for prosperity to all who enjoy them. So, flatter your friends with a dish of good wishes.

Egg Dumplings with Pork

Egg Dumplings With Pork

1	teaspoon dried shrimp
4	ounces (110g) finely chopped cooked pork
1	spring onion, thinly sliced
2	tablespoons soy sauce
1	tablespoon cornflour
1	tablespoon rice wine *or* dry sherry
1	clove garlic, minced*
6	fluid ounces (165ml) chicken broth
2	teaspoons cornflour
½	teaspoon caster sugar
4	eggs
	Cooking oil
1	teaspoon grated root ginger*
10	ounces (275g) torn fresh spinach
1	teaspoon sesame oil (optional)

In a small mixing bowl soak dried shrimp in enough hot water to cover for 30 minutes. Drain shrimp and chop finely.

For filling, in a small mixing bowl combine shrimp, pork, spring onion, *1 tablespoon* of the soy sauce, 1 tablespoon cornflour, rice wine or dry sherry, and garlic; mix well. Set aside.

For sauce, in a small mixing bowl combine remaining soy sauce, chicken broth, 2 teaspoons cornflour, and sugar; set aside. In a medium mixing bowl beat eggs.

Preheat a small frying pan over medium heat; add *2 teaspoons* cooking oil. For each dumpling, add *1 tablespoon* of the eggs. Using a spatula, shape egg into a 3- to 4-inch (7.5 to 10cm) circle (see photo 1). When egg is just set, place *1 rounded teaspoon* of the filling on half of the circle (see photo 2). Fold the other half over the filling (see photo 3). Press the edges together to seal. Remove dumpling. Repeat with remaining eggs and filling, making a total of 16 dumplings. (During cooking, it might be necessary to add more cooking oil to the pan.)

(See stir-frying photos, pages 24–25.) Heat a large frying pan over high heat. Add *1 tablespoon* cooking oil. Stir-fry root ginger for 15 seconds. Add spinach; stir-fry for 30 seconds. Sprinkle with sesame oil, if desired; stir-fry for 30 seconds to 1 minute more or just until limp (see photo 4). Arrange spinach around the edge of a serving dish; keep warm.

Return the large frying pan to high heat. Stir sauce; add to the frying pan. Cook and stir until thickened and bubbly; reduce heat to medium. Add dumplings. Stir gently to coat with sauce. Simmer, covered, for 1 to 2 minutes or until heated through. Spoon dumplings onto the centre of the serving dish. Makes 4 servings.

1 Using a spatula, shape the beaten egg into a thin circle, keeping the edges smooth and round. Work quickly before the egg sets.

2 When the egg is just set but still wet in appearance, spoon a little of the pork filling on half of the egg-circle in the frying pan.

*See cutting technique, page 27.

3 To fold each dumpling, use a spatula to quickly lift the unfilled half of the egg-circle over the filling, forming a half-circle.

4 When the spinach begins to appear limp, immediately remove it from the heat. The leaves should not be completely wilted.

Sensational Sushi

Introduce a popular Japanese tradition in your home—sushi. A delightful experience not soon forgotten, sushi, or "vinegared rice," is shaped and wrapped with fish or seaweed.

The Japanese use raw, cooked, or smoked fish and seafood to fashion a multitude of satisfying cold snacks. Two favourite versions we've chosen feature cooked prawns and smoked salmon.

Makizushi

Nigirizushi

Makizushi

Makizushi (MAH kee tsoo shee) means "rolled sushi."

2 recipes Vinegared Rice Omelette Roll
3 ounces (75g) sliced smoked red salmon
6 sheets nori seaweed (each about 8 inches (20cm) square)
1 small cucumber, seeded and cut into julienne strips* *or* 2 ounces (50g) fresh whole French beans, cooked
1 small carrot, cut into julienne strips* and cooked

Prepare Vinegared Rice and Omelette Roll. Cut salmon into ¼-inch (.5cm)-thick strips. To toast seaweed, place *each* sheet 5 to 6 inches (13 to 15cm) from the grill or hold over a gas range burner for 8 to 10 seconds on one side or until colour changes to green (see photo 2). Spread *about 4 ounces (110g)* of the rice over *each* sheet, spreading to within 1 inch (2.5cm) of *one* edge and to the other 3 edges.

Centre 3 or 4 salmon strips, an Omelette Roll, and/or vegetables on rice atop *each* seaweed sheet. Mix and match fillings. Starting opposite the side that has rice spread to within 1 inch (2.5cm) of the edge, roll up *each* sheet Swiss-roll style (see photo 3). Press edges together. Slice *each* roll into 6 pieces. Makes 36.

Vinegared Rice: Wash 4 ounces (110g) *short grain rice* under cold running water, rubbing grains together with fingers, until water runs clear. Drain. In a saucepan combine rice, 8 fluid ounces (220ml) *cold water,* and ¼ teaspoon *salt.* Bring to the boil; reduce heat to low and cover with a tight-fitting lid. Simmer 15 minutes. Remove from heat; stir in 4 teaspoons *rice vinegar or white vinegar,* 1 tablespoon *sugar,* and 1 tablespoon *mirin or dry sherry.* Cover; cool to room temperature. Makes 12 ounces (350g).

Omelette Roll: Beat 1 *egg* with 1 tablespoon *water.* Pour into a lightly greased 8-inch (20cm) frying pan; spread evenly. Cook over medium heat for 1½ to 2 minutes or until set. Do not turn. Remove from pan; cool. Trim omelette (see photo 1). Roll up Swiss-roll style. Makes 1.

1 When the omelette is thoroughly cooled, use a sharp knife or a cleaver to cut away two of its opposite curved edges so it resembles a rectangle.

2 To enhance the seaweed's flavour, lightly toast each sheet on one side only until the colour changes to green. Toasting it too long causes the seaweed to lose flavour and aroma.

3 To make Makizushi, roll the desired combination of fillings, rice, and toasted seaweed together Swiss-roll style. The stickiness of the rice mixture holds the roll together.

*See cutting technique, page 27.

Nigirizushi

Often made with cooked prawns called ebi, Nigirizushi (neeGEE ree tsoo shee) refers to sushi that is "pressed in the hand."

1 recipe Vinegared Rice (see recipe, opposite)
1 pound (450g) fresh *or* frozen medium prawns in shells (24 per pound)
2 tablespoons wasabi powder or horseradish sauce
1 tablespoon rice vinegar *or* white vinegar

Prepare Vinegared Rice; set aside. Thaw prawns, if frozen. To prevent prawns from curling, insert a wooden toothpick between the shell and the flesh on the underside of each prawn.

Bring 24 fluid ounces (680ml) *water* and 1 teaspoon *salt* to the boil; add prawns. Return to the boil; reduce heat and simmer, uncovered, for 1 to 3 minutes or until prawns turn pink, stirring occasionally. Rinse and drain; cool slightly. Remove toothpicks; peel and devein prawns, leaving tails intact (see tip, page 21). To butterfly prawns, make a deep slit along the back or the underside of each prawn; spread sides apart on a flat surface.

If using wasabi powder, in a small mixing bowl stir powder into 2 tablespoons *water;* set aside. In another small mixing bowl combine 4 fluid ounces (110ml) *water* and vinegar.

To shape rice, press a little rice firmly into a tablespoon. Invert onto greaseproof paper. (Moisten fingers with water-vinegar mixture as needed.) Shape rice into a ½-inch (1cm) -thick oval (see photo 1). Repeat with remaining rice, making a total of 24.

Using index finger, spread a *very thin* streak of wasabi mixture or horseradish sauce along the split side of *1* of the prawns (see photo 2). Place the prawn over rice oval, pressing the rice and prawn together. Repeat with the remaining prawns and rice.

To eat, turn upside down; dip only the prawn into *soy sauce*, if desired (see photo 3). Serve with *pink pickled ginger*, if desired. Makes 24.

1 To make Nigirizushi, shape the rice into a thick oval in one hand, using the fingers of your other hand. (For best results, prepare the rice only a few hours before shaping.)

2 Spread a small amount of the wasabi (wah SAH bee) mixture inside the open prawn. Known as Japanese horseradish, wasabi is appropriately called tears in sushi bars.

3 To enjoy Nigirizushi, dip only the prawn into the soy sauce. If the rice gets wet, it will crumble. Freshen your palate between bites of sushi with a little pink pickled ginger, if desired.

Over the Fire

Break out of your standard barbecue routine of burgers, chicken, and beef. Light a fire and add the flavour of the Orient to your outdoor cooking. The barbecue know-how is no different than for regular garden cooking. The difference is in the zesty marinades and spicy basting sauces.

To get you off to a blazing start, we show you how to skewer a saté, baste with sake, and dip into an exotic peanut sauce.

Thai Chicken Saté with Peanut Dipping Sauce

Thai Chicken Saté

Spicy satés call for cool, crisp relishes, such as Cucumber Salad (see recipe, page 66). Halve the salad or chill the extra to serve later.

6   **fluid ounces (165ml) Coconut Milk *or***
       tinned coconut milk (gata)
2   **cloves garlic, minced***
1   **tablespoon grated root ginger***
1   **tablespoon fish sauce**
1   **teaspoon finely grated lemon peel**
½   **teaspoon ground turmeric**
¼   **teaspoon ground coriander**
¼   **teaspoon crushed red pepper**
2   **whole large chicken breasts (about 2**
       pounds [900g] total), skinned and
       boned (see tip, page 34)
       Peanut Dipping Sauce (optional)
       (see recipe, right)

Soak 8 short bamboo skewers in hot water for at least 3 hours. (*Or,* use metal skewers and omit soaking.) Prepare Coconut Milk. For marinade, in a small mixing bowl combine Coconut Milk, garlic, root ginger, fish sauce, lemon peel, turmeric, coriander, and red pepper.

Cut chicken into 2x½-inch (5x2.5cm) strips. Loosely thread strips accordion-style onto the skewers (see photo 1). Place in a large shallow dish; pour marinade over all. Cover; marinate in the refrigerator for 2 hours, turning often and spooning marinade over chicken.

Pile briquettes into a pyramid in the centre of the firebox, then light. After heating, arrange the coals in a single layer (see photo 2). Test the temperature for *medium-hot* coals, using a 3-second count.

Meanwhile, prepare Peanut Dipping Sauce, if desired. Drain chicken, reserving marinade. Barbecue, uncovered, directly over *medium-hot* coals for 5 to 7 minutes or until chicken is tender, turning and brushing often with reserved marinade (see photo 3). Serve with Peanut Dipping Sauce, if desired. Makes 4 servings.

Coconut Milk: In a medium mixing bowl combine 8 fluid ounces (220ml) *boiling water* and 2 ounces (50g) desiccated *unsweetened coconut;*** let stand for 5 minutes. Place in a blender container or food processor bowl; cover and blend or process for 1 minute. Strain through cheesecloth, pressing mixture to squeeze out as much liquid as possible. Cover and store in the refrigerator for up to 3 days. Makes about 6 fluid ounces (165ml).

****Note:** Look for desiccated unsweetened coconut in Oriental markets or health food stores.

Peanut Dipping Sauce

Offer warm and pungent peanut dip with any of the satés in this chapter.

2½   **ounces (60g) chopped onion**
1   **clove garlic, minced***
2   **to 3 tablespoons cooking oil**
1   **tablespoon sweet soy sauce *or* Sweet**
       Soy Sauce (see tip, page 11)
1   **teaspoon tamarind paste**
½   **to 1 teaspoon Indonesian chilli paste**
       (sambal ulek) *or* Oriental chilli paste
½   **teaspoon shrimp paste *or* anchovy**
       paste
6   **ounces (175g) smooth peanut butter**
       Chopped peanuts (optional)

In a small saucepan cook onion and garlic in *1 tablespoon* of the hot oil over medium-high heat until tender but not brown, stirring often. In a small mixing bowl combine sweet soy sauce, tamarind paste, chilli paste, and shrimp paste or anchovy paste. Stir into onion mixture.

Add peanut butter. Reduce heat to low. Cook and stir until smooth and heated through. Stir in enough of the remaining oil to make of desired consistency. Sprinkle with peanuts, if desired. Serve warm. Makes about 8 ounces (220ml).

*See cutting technique, page 27.

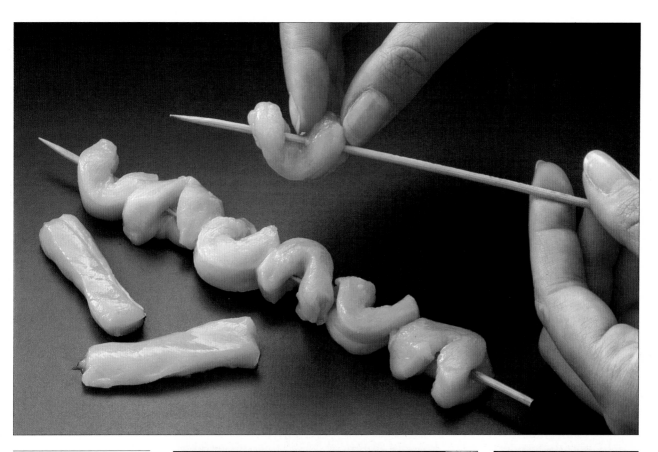

1 For even cooking, loosely thread the meat strips or seafood onto the damp bamboo skewers, as shown. Soaking the wooden skewers in hot water keeps them from burning on the barbecue.

2 When the coals appear ash grey, arrange them in a single layer. Then, test the temperature. Hold your hand, palm down, at the level the food will cook.

Start counting "1,001, 1,002," and so forth. If you need to remove your hand after 2 seconds, the coals are *hot;* if you reach 3 seconds, they're *medium-hot.*

3 Brush the meat or seafood with a marinade or basting sauce to add flavour and keep it moist as it cooks. Use a long-handled brush to protect your hands from the heat.

Indonesian Chicken Saté

Sweet soy, known as ketjap manis, is thicker than the soy sauce you buy at the supermarket, and it has a flavour like black treacle.

Cucumber Salad (optional)
  (see recipe, right)
4 fluid ounces (110ml) sweet soy sauce
    or Sweet Soy Sauce (see tip,
    page 11)
½ teaspoon finely grated lime peel
2 fluid ounces (55ml) lime juice
2 cloves garlic, minced*
2 whole large chicken breasts (about 2
    pounds [900g] total), skinned and
    boned (see tip, page 34)
4 chicken thighs, skinned and boned
  Peanut Dipping Sauce (optional)
    (see recipe, page 64)
  Lime *or* lemon wedges (optional)
  Saté condiments (optional)
    Ground black pepper
    Chopped spring onions
    Seeded and chopped red and green
      chilli peppers (see Note, page 30)

Soak 16 short bamboo skewers in hot water for at least 3 hours. (*Or,* use metal skewers and omit soaking.) Prepare Cucumber Salad, if desired. For marinade, in a small mixing bowl combine sweet soy sauce, lime peel, lime juice, and garlic; set aside.

Cut chicken into 2x½-inch (5x1cm) strips. Loosely thread strips accordion-style onto the skewers (see photo 1, page 65). Place in a shallow dish; pour marinade over all. Cover; marinate in the refrigerator for 2 hours, turning often and spooning marinade over chicken.

Pile briquettes into a pyramid in the centre of the firebox, then light. After heating, arrange the coals in a single layer (see photo 2, page 65). Test the temperature for *medium-hot* coals, using a 3-second count.

Meanwhile, prepare Peanut Dipping Sauce, if desired. Drain chicken, reserving marinade. Barbecue, uncovered, directly over *medium-hot* coals for 5 to 7 minutes or until chicken is tender, turning and brushing often with reserved marinade (see photo 3, page 65).

To serve, arrange skewers on a serving dish; squeeze lime or lemon wedges over chicken, if desired. Dip into Peanut Dipping Sauce and top with desired condiments. Serve with Cucumber Salad, if desired. Makes 8 servings.

Cucumber Salad

2 medium cucumbers
2 thinly sliced spring onions
1 red chilli pepper, seeded and finely
    chopped (see Note, page 30)
8 fluid ounces (220ml) rice vinegar *or*
    white vinegar
3 fluid ounces (80ml) water
1½ ounces (40g) caster sugar
1 clove garlic, minced*
¼ teaspoon salt
¼ teaspoon ground turmeric

Halve unpeeled cucumbers lengthwise, then thinly slice cucumbers crosswise. In a shallow dish combine cucumbers, spring onions, and chilli pepper; set aside.

For marinade, in a small mixing bowl combine rice vinegar or white vinegar, water, sugar, garlic, salt, and turmeric. Stir until sugar dissolves. Pour over cucumber mixture. Cover and marinate in the refrigerator for at least 2 hours, stirring occasionally. Store in the refrigerator for up to 3 days. Drain before serving. Serves 8.

*See cutting technique, page 27.

Barbecued Scallops

A Japanese snack glazed with a sweetened sake sauce.

1 **pound (450g) fresh *or* frozen scallops**
2 **fluid ounces (55ml) sake**
2 **fluid ounces (55ml) soy sauce**
1 **tablespoon caster sugar**
 Lemon wedges (optional)

Soak 6 short bamboo skewers in hot water for at least 4 hours. (*Or,* use metal skewers and omit soaking.) Thaw scallops, if frozen.

Meanwhile, for basting sauce, in a small saucepan combine sake, soy sauce, and sugar; bring to the boil. Boil for 2 minutes or until sauce measures 3 fluid ounces (80ml), stirring occasionally; set aside.

Pile briquettes into a pyramid in the centre of the firebox, then light. After heating, arrange the coals in a single layer (see photo 2, page 65). Test the temperature for *hot* coals, using a 2-second count.

Halve large scallops. Rinse; pat dry with kitchen papers. Thread scallops onto the skewers, allowing a ¼-inch (.5cm) space between pieces (see photo 1, page 65). Barbecue, uncovered, directly over *hot* coals about 10 minutes or until scallops are opaque, turning and brushing often with basting sauce (see photo 3, page 65). Serve with lemon wedges and any remaining sauce, if desired. Makes 6 appetizer servings.

Prawns Saté

Spicy and aromatic, this saté is popular in Malaysia.

1 **pound (450g) fresh *or* frozen prawns in shells**
2 **tablespoons sliced spring onion**
1 **clove garlic, minced***
2 **teaspoons cooking oil**
6 **fluid ounces (165ml) chicken broth**
3 **tablespoons peanut butter**
1 **tablespoon soy sauce**
½ **teaspoon finely grated lemon peel**
1 **tablespoon lemon juice**
1 **teaspoon chilli powder**
½ **teaspoon soft brown sugar**
¼ **teaspoon ground ginger**

Soak 8 short bamboo skewers in hot water for at least 3 hours. (*Or,* use metal skewers and omit soaking.) Thaw prawns, if frozen. For marinade, in a small saucepan cook spring onion and garlic in hot oil over medium heat for 1 minute, stirring often. Stir in broth, peanut butter, soy sauce, lemon peel, lemon juice, chilli powder, brown sugar, and ginger. Bring to boiling; reduce heat. Simmer, uncovered, for 10 minutes; stir often. Remove from heat; cool.

Peel prawns, leaving tails attached; devein (see tip, page 21). Rinse; pat dry with kitchen papers. Place prawns in a shallow dish; pour marinade over all. Cover and marinate in the refrigerator for 2 hours, stirring prawns occasionally.

Pile briquettes into a pyramid in the centre of the firebox, then light. After heating, arrange the coals in a single layer (see photo 2, page 65). Test the temperature for *medium-hot* coals, using a 3-second count.

Drain prawns, reserving marinade. Thread prawns onto skewers, allowing a ¼-inch (.5cm) space between pieces (see photo 1, page 65). Barbecue, uncovered, directly over *medium-hot* coals for 10 to 12 minutes or until prawns turn pink, turning and brushing often with reserved marinade (see photo 3, page 65). Heat remaining marinade and pass with prawns. Serves 4.

Steam Cooking

Take a cue from Far Eastern cooks, and steam fish, poultry, meats, vegetables, breads, even desserts. A Chinese cooking method as old as their civilisation, steaming preserves the flavour, colour, shape, and nutrients of food without adding extra calories.

To help broaden your repertoire of steamed foods, check the next few pages for new and delicious ideas.

*Malaysian Fish
with Hot Chilli Sauce*

Malaysian Fish with Hot Chilli Sauce

1½ to 2 pounds (700 to 900g) fresh *or* frozen
     dressed whitefish *or* other fish with
     head and tail
     Spring Onion Brushes (optional)
     (see tip, opposite)
2   tablespoons fish sauce
6   ounces (175g) shredded lettuce
4   fluid ounces (110ml) chicken broth
1   tablespoon caster sugar
1   tablespoon vinegar
1   tablespoon rice wine *or* dry sherry
2   teaspoons cornflour
1   tablespoon grated root ginger*
1   tablespoon cooking oil
2   spring onions, thinly sliced
1   red chilli pepper, seeded and finely
     chopped (see Note, page 30)
¼   to ½ teaspoon crushed red pepper *or*
     ⅛ to ¼ teaspoon ground red pepper

Thaw fish, if frozen. If desired, remove head and tail. Rinse and pat dry with kitchen papers; weigh fish. Score fish with 6 diagonal cuts on one side (see photo 1). Brush *half* of the fish sauce on fish and in cuts; set aside. Prepare Spring Onion Brushes, if desired.

In a steamer place a greased steamer rack over water (see photo 2). Bring water to the boil over high heat. Place fish on the rack (see photo 3). Cover; steam until fish flakes easily with a fork. Allow 6 to 9 minutes for each ½ pound (225g) of fish. Transfer to a serving dish; keep warm. Place lettuce on the rack. Cover; steam for 1 to 2 minutes or just until limp. Spoon around fish.

In a small mixing bowl mix broth, sugar, vinegar, rice wine or dry sherry, cornflour, and remaining fish sauce. In a medium saucepan cook root ginger in hot oil for 15 seconds. Add sliced spring onions; cook for 1 minute. Stir in chilli and red pepper. Stir broth mixture; add to the saucepan. Cook and stir until thickened and bubbly. Cook and stir 2 minutes more. Pour some sauce over fish; pass remaining sauce. Garnish with onion brushes, if desired. Serves 3.

See cutting technique, page 27.

1 Use a sharp knife to make the cuts almost through to the bone. This type of scoring allows the seasonings to seep into the flesh of the fish.

2 Add water to the steamer, then place the rack in the steamer to check the water level. (The water should not touch the steamer rack when it boils.)

When the rack doesn't have sides, as shown, place it in the steamer before the water begins to boil (see tip, page 74).

3 Place the food on the rack so the steam can circulate freely in the steamer.

Spring Onion Brushes: Trim spring onions. For *each* brush, insert a sharp knife 2 to 3 inches (5 to 7.5cm) from one end of the onion. Cut toward the nearest end. Rotate onion; repeat the cut until end is in slivers. If desired, repeat on other end. Chill in ice water about 30 minutes or until curled.

Beef and Cabbage Rolls

Indonesian cooks favour banana leaves to encase a boldly seasoned beef mixture, but we've used an edible wrapper of cabbage leaves.

6   **fluid ounces (165ml) Coconut Milk (see recipe, page 64)**
1   **tablespoon cooking oil**
1   **small onion, finely chopped**
2   **cloves garlic, minced***
1   **tablespoon grated root ginger***
1   **stalk fresh lemongrass, chopped (1 tablespoon), *or* 1 teaspoon finely grated lemon peel**
4   **macadamia nuts *or* blanched almonds, finely chopped**
1   **pound (450g) minced beef**
1   **tablespoon tamarind paste**
1   **teaspoon ground coriander**
½   **teaspoon crushed red pepper *or* ¼ teaspoon ground red pepper**
¼   **teaspoon salt**
¼   **teaspoon ground cumin**
16 **medium cabbage leaves**
3   **hard-boiled eggs, sliced**
    Hot cooked rice (optional)
    Sweet Soy Dipping Sauce (optional) (see recipe, right)

Prepare Coconut Milk. *(See stir-frying photos, pages 24–25 and 30–31.)* Preheat a wok or large frying pan over high heat; add oil. Stir-fry onion, garlic, root ginger, lemongrass or lemon peel, and nuts for 1 minute. Remove onion mixture from the wok.

Crumble *half* of the minced beef in the hot wok or frying pan. Stir-fry for 3 minutes. Remove beef; drain off fat. Stir-fry remaining beef for 3 minutes. Drain. Return all beef to the wok; stir in onion mixture, Coconut Milk, tamarind paste, coriander, red pepper, salt, and cumin. Reduce heat; simmer, uncovered, about 5 minutes or until most of the liquid has evaporated, stirring occasionally. Remove from heat; cool.

Remove the centre veins of cabbage leaves, keeping each leaf in 1 piece. Immerse leaves in boiling water about 3 minutes or until limp; drain.

To make rolls, place 1 or 2 slices hard-boiled egg on 1 cabbage leaf; top with *2 slightly rounded tablespoons* of the meat mixture. Fold in sides. Starting at one of the unfolded ends, roll up leaf, tucking in folded sides as you roll. Repeat with remaining egg slices, cabbage leaves, and meat mixture.

In a steamer place a steamer rack over water (see photo 2, page 70). Bring water to the boil over high heat. Place rolls on the rack so the sides do not touch (see photo 3, page 70). (Cover and chill rolls that don't fit on the rack.) Cover and steam about 20 minutes or until heated through. Repeat with remaining rolls.

Meanwhile, prepare Sweet Soy Dipping Sauce, if desired. Serve rolls with rice and drizzle with Sweet Soy Dipping Sauce, if desired. Makes 16.

Sweet Soy Dipping Sauce

2   **fluid ounces (55ml) lime juice**
3   **tablespoons water**
3   **tablespoons sweet soy sauce *or* Sweet Soy Sauce (see tip, page 11)**
½   **to 1 teaspoon Indonesian chilli paste (sambal ulek) *or* Oriental chilli paste**

In a small mixing bowl combine lime juice, water, sweet soy sauce, and chilli paste. Makes about 5 fluid ounces (140ml).

*See cutting technique, page 27.

Steamed Chicken And Vegetables

Pass the fish sauce for an extra dash of flavour.

2 whole medium chicken breasts (about 1½ pounds [700g]), skinned and boned (see tip, page 34)
1 medium cucumber, peeled, seeded, and cut into 1-inch (2.5cm) pieces
1 medium courgette, bias-sliced ¼ inch (.5cm) thick*
4 spring onions, bias-sliced into 1-inch (2.5cm) pieces*
2 tablespoons fish sauce
1 teaspoon caster sugar
½ teaspoon ground laos *or* ¼ teaspoon ground ginger
⅛ to ¼ teaspoon pepper
2 medium tomatoes, cut into wedges
1 tablespoon snipped cilantro *or* parsley
Hot cooked rice (optional)
Fish sauce (optional)

Cut chicken into 1-inch (2.5cm) cubes (see tip, page 35). In an 8x1½-inch (20x4cm) round baking dish combine chicken, cucumber, courgette, and spring onions. (Make sure the baking dish is at least 1 inch (2.5cm) smaller than the steamer rack.) In a small mixing bowl combine 2 tablespoons fish sauce, sugar, laos or ginger, and pepper; pour over chicken mixture. Cover the dish with foil.

In a steamer place a steamer rack over water (see photo 2, page 70). Bring water to the boil over high heat. Place the baking dish on the steamer rack (see photo 3, page 70). Cover and steam for 20 to 25 minutes or until chicken is done. Uncover; stir chicken and vegetables. Top with tomatoes and cilantro or parsley. Cover and steam for 1 to 2 minutes more or until tomato is heated through. Serve with rice and additional fish sauce, if desired. Serves 4.

Microwave Directions: Cut chicken and vegetables as above. In a medium round microwave-safe casserole combine chicken, cucumber, courgette, and spring onions. In a small mixing bowl combine 2 tablespoons fish sauce, sugar, laos or ginger, and pepper; pour over chicken mixture. Micro-cook, covered, on 100% power (HIGH) for 7 to 9 minutes or until chicken is tender and vegetables are crisp-tender, stirring after every 2 minutes. Top with tomatoes and cilantro or parsley. Cook, covered, on high for 1 to 2 minutes more or until tomatoes are heated through. Serve with rice and additional fish sauce, if desired.

Attention, Microwave Owners!

The microwave timings in this book were tested using countertop microwave ovens with 600 to 700 watts of cooking power. The cooking times are approximate because microwave ovens vary by manufacturer.

Lotus Leaf Buns

7 **to 8 ounces (200 to 225g) plain flour**
1 **packet dried yeast***
4 **fluid ounces (110ml) milk**
2 **tablespoons lard**
1 **tablespoon caster sugar**
1 **teaspoon sesame oil *or* cooking oil**

In a small mixing bowl combine *2½ ounces (60g)* of the flour and yeast. In a small saucepan heat milk, lard, sugar, and ¼ teaspoon *salt* just until warm (115°F or 46°C) and lard is almost melted, stirring constantly. Add to flour mixture. Beat with an electric mixer on low speed for 30 seconds, scraping the bowl constantly. Beat on high speed for 3 minutes. Stir in as much of the remaining flour as you can.

On a lightly floured surface knead in enough of the remaining flour to make a moderately stiff dough that is smooth and elastic (6 to 8 minutes). Shape into a ball. Place in a greased bowl; turn once to grease surface. Cover and let rise in a warm place until double (about 1 hour).

Punch dough down; divide into 10 balls. Cover and let rest for 10 minutes. Flatten *each* ball into a 3-inch (7.5cm) circle. For *each* bun, lightly brush *half* of the circle with sesame or cooking oil. Fold in half to form a semicircle; press edges together to seal. Using a sharp knife, make 2 evenly spaced cuts, ½ inch (1cm) deep, on the rounded edge. Make shallow cuts in a crisscross pattern atop bun. Place on a greased baking tray. Repeat with remaining circles. Cover; let rise in a warm place for 15 minutes.

In a steamer place a greased steamer rack over water (see photo 2, page 70). Bring water to the boil over high heat. Place buns on the rack so the sides do not touch (see photo 3, page 70). (Cover and chill buns that don't fit on the rack.) Cover and steam about 15 minutes or until buns spring back when touched. Repeat with remaining buns. Serve warm. Makes 10.

***Note:** Quick-rising active dried yeast is not recommended for this recipe.

Successful Steaming

When you don't have a steamer, improvise. Assemble your own using a large wok or a covered casserole.

Choosing the Rack
For a steamer rack, use a round wire cooling rack, a small metal colander, or a foil pie plate with holes poked in the bottom.

Supporting the Rack
The sloping sides of the wok hold the rack above the water. To support the rack in a covered casserole, invert 3 or 4 custard cups in the tin. Add about 1 inch (2.5cm) of water, then place the rack on top of the inverted cups.

Adding the Rack
A rack with sides that are easy to grasp should be filled with food, then placed in the steamer over boiling water. A rack without sides should be placed in the steamer before the water boils. Then, add the food after the water boils.

Adding Water
Check the water level in the steamer as the food cooks. Add more boiling water, as needed. Do not remove the lid during cooking, unless checking the water level or doneness of the food. When you do need to lift the lid, tilt it away from you to allow the steam to escape without burning you.

Steamed Orange Roll

A yummy orange filling swirls throughout a light and delicate Cantonese sweet.

2 eggs
½ teaspoon grated orange peel
1 or 2 drops vanilla essence
2 ounces (50g) caster sugar
2½ ounces (60g) plain flour
Icing sugar
10 ounces (275g) orange marmalade
1 tablespoon lemon juice
1 ounce (25g) toasted chopped almonds
Toasted sliced almonds

In a steamer place a 12-inch (30cm) *bamboo* steamer rack over water (see photo 2, page 70). Remove the rack and line it with silver foil, making sure the bottom and sides are covered with a single sheet of foil; trim off excess paper.

In a small mixing bowl beat eggs, orange peel, vanilla essence, and ⅛ teaspoon *salt* with an electric mixer on medium speed for 1 minute. Gradually add sugar, beating on high speed about 5 minutes or until mixture is thick and lemon coloured and sugar is dissolved. Fold flour into egg mixture. Spread evenly on prepared rack.

Bring water in the steamer to the boil over high heat. Place the rack over boiling water. Cover the rack with a clean dish towel, then cover with the steamer lid. Steam about 4 minutes or until cake tests done. Remove the rack. Invert onto another dry towel sprinkled with icing sugar; do not remove paper. Cool.

For filling, reserve *1 tablespoon* of the marmalade. Mix remaining marmalade, lemon juice, and chopped nuts. Remove paper from cake. Spread filling over cake to within ½ inch (1cm) of the edge. Roll up Swiss-roll style. Wrap in sugar-sprinkled towel. Let stand for 30 minutes. To garnish, place cake seam side down on a serving dish; sprinkle with icing sugar. Spread reserved marmalade in 3 evenly spaced 1½-inch (4cm) circles atop cake. Arrange sliced nuts around circles to resemble flowers. Serves 12.

Steamed Eggs With Mushrooms

Savour the tang of Nuoc Cham (Vietnamese table sauce) with this tasty brunch or supper dish.

½ ounce (10g) bean threads
Nuoc Cham (see recipe, page 40)
1 tablespoon cooking oil
2 spring onions, thinly sliced
4 ounces (110g) minced pork
7 ounces (200g) tinned straw mushrooms, drained and sliced
1 tablespoon fish sauce
⅛ teaspoon pepper
6 beaten eggs
Hot cooked rice (optional)

In a medium mixing bowl soak bean threads in enough hot water to cover for 30 minutes. Drain well; squeeze out excess moisture. Cut into 2-inch (5cm) lengths (see photo 1, page 18). Meanwhile, prepare Nuoc Cham.

(See stir-frying photos, pages 24–25 and 30–31.) Preheat a wok or medium frying pan over high heat; add oil. Stir-fry spring onions in hot oil for 1 minute. Crumble minced pork in the hot wok or frying pan. Stir-fry about 3 minutes or until pork is no longer pink. Remove from heat; drain off fat. Stir in bean threads, straw mushrooms, fish sauce, and pepper. Cool.

In a steamer place a steamer rack over water (see photo 2, page 70). Bring water to the boil over high heat. In a greased medium round baking dish combine beaten eggs and cooled pork mixture; cover the dish with foil. (Make sure the baking dish is at least 1 inch [2.5cm] smaller than the steamer rack.)

Place the dish on the steamer rack (see photo 3, page 70). Cover and steam about 15 minutes or until the edge is done but the centre is not quite set. Immediately remove from the steamer. Let stand for 5 to 10 minutes or until the centre is set. Serve with rice, if desired. Pass Nuoc Cham. Makes 4 servings.

Silver-Thread Buns

Fancy steamed buns or breads often replace rice at Chinese holiday meals or banquets. A popular choice for such meals is silver-thread buns.

Also called snail buns, silver-thread buns are ingeniously fashioned from thread-like strands of dough to resemble a snail shell. They delight the palate as well as the eye.

Steamed Silver-Thread Buns

Steamed Silver-Thread Buns

Chinese cooks prefer lard for their dough making; you'll find butter or margarine gives you the same delicious flavour and texture.

14 **to 16 ounces (400 to 450g) plain flour**
1 **packet dried yeast***
8 **fluid ounces (220ml) water**
2 **tablespoons caster sugar**
1 **tablespoon butter, margarine, *or* lard**
¼ **teaspoon salt**
2 **ounces (50g) butter, margarine, *or* lard, softened**
2 **tablespoons caster sugar**
Black sesame seed (optional)

In a small mixing bowl combine *6 ounces (175g)* of the flour and yeast. In a small saucepan heat water; 2 tablespoons sugar; 1 tablespoon butter, margarine, or lard; and salt just until warm (115°F or 46°C) and butter, margarine, or lard is almost melted, stirring constantly. Add to flour mixture.

Beat with an electric mixer on low speed for 30 seconds, scraping the bowl constantly. Beat on high speed for 3 minutes. Using a spoon, stir in as much of the remaining flour as you can.

On a lightly floured surface knead in enough of the remaining flour to make a moderately stiff dough that is smooth and elastic (6 to 8 minutes). Shape into a ball. Place in a greased bowl; turn once to grease surface. Cover and let rise in a warm place until double (about 1 hour). Meanwhile, combine 2 ounces (50g) butter, margarine, or lard and 2 tablespoons sugar; set aside.

Punch dough down; cover and let rest for 10 minutes. On a lightly floured surface roll dough into a 20x9-inch (50x23cm) rectangle. Spread sugar mixture over dough. Fold dough in thirds, forming a 20x3-inch (50x7.5cm) rectangle. Slice dough crosswise into very thin threads, *each* ⅛ to ¼ inch (3mm to .5cm) wide (see photo 1).

For *each* bun, gently stretch a group of 8 threads from both ends until about 7 inches (18cm) long (see photo 2). Starting at one end, wrap threads in a spiral around the first 2 fingers, stretching dough slightly (see photo 3). Tuck the other end into the top to seal as you remove bun from fingers and place on a lightly greased baking tray (see photo 4). Repeat with remaining dough. If desired, sprinkle with black sesame seed. Cover; let rise in a warm place for 20 minutes.

In a steamer place a greased steamer rack over water (see photo 2, page 70). Bring water to the boil over high heat. Place buns on the steamer rack so the sides do not touch (see photo 3, page 70). (Cover and chill buns that don't fit on the rack.) Cover and steam for 10 to 15 minutes or until buns spring back when touched. Repeat steaming with remaining buns. Serve warm. Makes about 12.

***Note:** Quick-rising active dried yeast is not recommended for this recipe.

1 On a lightly floured surface, slice the folded dough crosswise into very thin threads or strands, using a sharp cleaver or a large knife.

2 Divide the folded threads or strands into groups of eight. Then, holding the opposite ends of each group of threads together, gently stretch or pull the threads lengthwise until they are about 7 inches (18cm) long, as shown.

3 Wrap one end of the group of dough threads around the first two fingers of one hand. Continue wrapping the dough around fingers in a spiral, slightly stretching dough as you wrap.

4 When you reach the other end of the threads, use your thumb to tuck the end into the centre of the bun. At the same time, slide the bun off your fingers onto a lightly greased baking tray.

Deep-Fried Favourites

Light and lacy tempura . . .
crispy sweet and sour pork
. . . luscious lemon chicken.
Each of these crisp-fried
Oriental delicacies is a well-
known classic. The key to
their popularity? A special
batter that deep-fries to
tender perfection without
masking the natural flavour
of the food.

Tempura

Tempura

12 **ounces (350g) fresh *or* frozen shelled
medium prawns (see tip, page 21)
or scallops**

1 **small sweet potato, peeled and sliced
¼ inch (.5cm) thick**

3 **ounces (75g) halved fresh mushrooms
or 1-inch (2.5cm) cubed aubergine**

3 **ounces (75g) fresh French beans *or*
fresh asparagus, cut into 2-inch
(5cm) pieces**

3 **spring onions, cut into 2-inch
(5cm) pieces**

8 **parsley sprigs
Tempura Dipping Sauce
Tempura condiments (optional)
Grated root ginger***
Grated daikon*
**Lemon *or* lime wedges
Cooking oil for deep-fat frying**

1 **slightly beaten egg yolk**

8 **fluid ounces (220ml) ice water**

5 **ounces (150g) plain flour**

Thaw prawns or scallops, if frozen; rinse. Using kitchen papers, thoroughly dry seafood, vegetables, and parsley. Prepare Tempura Dipping Sauce and Tempura condiments. In a wok, deep-fat fryer, or saucepan, heat 1½ to 2 inches (4 to 5cm) oil to 365°F (185°C) (see photo 1).

Just before frying, prepare batter. In a medium mixing bowl mix egg yolk and ice water. Add flour; stir just until combined (see photo 2).

To serve, give each person a small bowl of sauce. Pass condiments; add to sauce, as desired. Dip seafood, vegetables, and parsley into batter (see photo 3). Fry, a few pieces at a time, for 2 to 3 minutes or until light golden, turning once. Remove from oil; drain well (see photo 4). Dip into sauce mixture. Makes 6 servings.

Tempura Dipping Sauce: In a saucepan combine 8 fluid ounces (220ml) *Dashi* (see recipe, page 20), 2 fluid ounces (55ml) *sake or dry sherry,* 2 fluid ounces (55ml) *soy sauce,* and 1 teaspoon *caster sugar.* Bring to the boil; stir until sugar dissolves. Serve warm. Makes 12 fluid ounces (330ml).

*See cutting technique, page 27.

1 Always check the temperature of the oil, using a deep-fat frying thermometer. Just be sure the bulb doesn't touch the saucepan.

If the temperature of the oil is too low, the food will become greasy; if it's too high, the food will turn dark before it's done.

2 Use a spoon for mixing the tempura batter. Take care not to overmix or the batter will not puff. (A few lumps may remain.) For other batters, use a rotary beater and beat the mixture until smooth.

3 Dip the food into the batter, then allow the excess to drip back into the bowl, as shown. Fry only a few pieces at a time to keep them from sticking together in the hot oil.

4 Use a wire skimmer or a slotted spoon to remove deep-fried pieces of food from the oil. Drain on a wok rack, as shown, or on kitchen paper.

Cantonese Lemon Chicken

2 **large chicken breasts (about 2 pounds [900g] total), skinned and boned**
8 **fluid ounces (220ml) chicken broth**
2 **tablespoons caster sugar**
1 **tablespoon cornflour**
2 **teaspoons finely grated lemon peel**
3 **tablespoons lemon juice**
  Cooking oil for deep-fat frying
1 **beaten egg**
1 **ounce (25g) cornflour**
1½ **ounces (40g) plain flour**
2 **fluid ounces (55ml) water**
½ **teaspoon salt**
1 **tablespoon cooking oil**
3 **spring onions, bias-sliced into 1-inch [2.5cm] pieces***
1 **teaspoon sesame oil (optional)**
3½ **ounces (85g) shredded lettuce**

Cut chicken into 1-inch (2.5cm) cubes (see tip, page 35). For sauce, in a mixing bowl combine chicken broth, sugar, 1 tablespoon cornflour, lemon peel, and lemon juice; set aside.

In a wok, deep-fat fryer, or medium saucepan, heat 1½ to 2 inches (4 to 5cm) cooking oil to 365°F (185°C) (see photo 1, page 82). Meanwhile, for batter, in a small mixing bowl mix egg, cornflour, flour, water, and salt; beat until smooth, using a rotary beater (see photo 2, page 82). Dip chicken into batter (see photo 3, page 82). Fry 6 or 7 pieces at a time about 4 minutes or until golden brown, turning once. Remove from oil and drain (see photo 4, page 83). Keep warm in a 300°F (150°C) gas mark 2 oven while frying remaining chicken.

(See stir-frying photos, pages 24–25 and 30–31.) Preheat a wok or frying pan over high heat; add 1 tablespoon cooking oil. Stir-fry spring onions in hot oil for 1 minute or until crisp-tender. Push from the centre of the wok. Stir sauce; add to the centre of the wok or frying pan. Cook and stir until thickened and bubbly. Cook and stir for 2 minutes more. Add deep-fried chicken and sesame oil, if desired; stir together to coat with sauce. Serve over lettuce. Makes 4 servings.

*See cutting technique, page 27.

Deep-Fried Phoenix-Tailed Prawns

A mythical bird, the phoenix is a symbol of beauty and the inspiration for many Chinese dishes.

1 **pound (450g) fresh or frozen jumbo prawns in shells (about 16)**
1½ **ounces (40g) plain flour**
1 **ounce (25g) cornflour**
1 **teaspoon baking powder**
1 **teaspoon grated root ginger***
½ **teaspoon salt**
  Szechwan Pepper-Salt (optional)
  Cooking oil for deep-fat frying

Thaw prawns, if frozen. For batter, in a mixing bowl mix flour, cornflour, baking powder, root ginger, salt, and 8 fluid ounces (220ml) *water*; beat with a rotary beater until smooth (see photo 2, page 82). Cover; let stand for 30 to 45 minutes. If desired, prepare Szechwan Pepper-Salt.

Meanwhile, peel and devein prawns, leaving tails intact (see tip, page 21). To prevent prawns from curling, make 5 or 6 cuts crosswise on the underside of prawns, cutting to, but not through, backs of prawns. Place, cut side down, on kitchen paper. (Prawns should lie flat.)

In a wok, deep-fat fryer, or medium saucepan, heat 1½ to 2 inches (4 to 5cm) cooking oil to 365°F (185°C) (see photo 1, page 82). Dip prawns into batter (see photo 3, page 82). Fry prawns, a few at a time, for 1½ minutes or until golden brown, turning once. Remove from oil and drain (see photo 4, page 83). Keep warm in a 300°F (150°C) gas mark 2 oven while frying remaining prawns. Serve with Szechwan Pepper-Salt, if desired. Makes 8 appetizer servings or 4 main-dish servings.

Szechwan Pepper-Salt: In a small saucepan mix 3 tablespoons whole *Szechwan peppers or* whole *black peppers* and 1 teaspoon *salt*. Cook over medium heat, stirring constantly, about 3 minutes or until peppers begin to smoke and salt is light brown. Remove from heat; cool. Using a mortar and pestle or a rolling pin, crush mixture. Pass through a sieve. Store in a tightly covered jar. Makes 3 tablespoons.

Sweet and Sour Pork

A yummy Cantonese dish that pairs the sweetness of sugar with the tanginess of vinegar.

1 **pound (450g) boneless pork**
3 **tablespoons cornflour**
1 **tablespoon rice wine *or* dry sherry**
1 **tablespoon soy sauce**
8 **ounces (225g) pineapple chunks (juice pack)**
3 **tablespoons vinegar**
2 **tablespoons caster sugar**
2 **tablespoons tomato puree**
1 **tablespoon cornflour**
2 **teaspoons soy sauce**
½ **teaspoon sesame oil (optional)**
  Cooking oil for deep-fat frying
1 **beaten egg**
2½ **ounces (60g) plain flour**
2 **fluid ounces (55ml) water**
¼ **teaspoon salt**
1 **tablespoon cooking oil**
1 **clove garlic, minced**
1 **carrot, cut into julienne strips**
1 **large green pepper, cut into 1-inch (2.5cm) squares**

Cut pork into 1-inch (2.5cm) cubes. For marinade, in a medium mixing bowl combine 3 tablespoons cornflour, rice wine or dry sherry, and 1 tablespoon soy sauce; stir in pork. Cover and let stand at room temperature for 30 minutes, stirring occasionally. (*Or,* marinate in the refrigerator for 2 hours.)

Meanwhile, drain pineapple, reserving juice. Add water to reserved juice to make 5 fluid ounces (140ml). For sauce, in a mixing bowl combine juice mixture, vinegar, sugar, tomato puree, cornflour, 2 teaspoons soy sauce, and sesame oil, if desired. Set aside.

In a wok, deep-fat fryer, or medium saucepan, heat 1½ to 2 inches (4 to 5cm) cooking oil to 365°F (185°C) (see photo 1, page 82).

Meanwhile, for batter, in a small mixing bowl combine egg, flour, 2 fluid ounces (55ml) water, and salt; beat until smooth, using a rotary beater (see photo 2, page 82).

Dip pork into batter (see photo 3, page 82). Fry pork, 5 or 6 pieces at a time, for 5 to 6 minutes or until golden brown, turning once. Remove from oil and drain (see photo 4, page 83). Keep deep-fried pork warm in a 300°F (150°C) gas mark 2 oven while frying remaining pork.

(See stir-frying photos, pages 24–25 and 30–31.) Preheat a wok or large frying pan over high heat; add 1 tablespoon cooking oil. Stir-fry garlic in hot oil for 15 seconds. Add carrot; stir-fry for 1½ minutes. Add green pepper; stir-fry about 1 minute or until vegetables are crisp-tender. Push from the centre of the wok.

Stir sauce; add to the centre of the wok or frying pan. Cook and stir until thickened and bubbly. Cook and stir for 2 minutes more. Add pineapple; stir ingredients together to coat with sauce. Stir in deep-fried pork; serve immediately. Makes 4 servings.

Versatile Wontons

Wontons add a lively and versatile note to any Oriental menu. Just vary the filling and cooking method to suit your needs.

When the menu calls for soup, tuck a savoury filling inside the wontons and simmer in a flavoursome broth.

Need a party snack? Deep-fry sweet or savoury filled wontons until they are crisp and crunchy.

Wonton Soup

Wonton Soup

An excellent make-ahead soup. Fill the wontons and freeze. When you're hungry for soup, add the frozen wontons to the hot broth and cook about 8 minutes.

Pork and Prawn Filling
36 **wonton wrappers *or* 9 egg roll wrappers, cut into quarters**
64 **fluid ounces (1.8l) chicken broth**
 2 **tablespoons rice wine *or* dry sherry**
 2 **tablespoons soy sauce**
 1 **teaspoon sesame oil (optional)**
 8 **ounces (225g) torn fresh spinach**

Prepare Pork and Prawn Filling. For wontons, place *1* wonton or egg roll wrapper with 1 point toward you. Top with *1 rounded teaspoon* of the filling just off-centre (see photo 1). Fold the nearest point of wrapper over filling, tucking the point under filling (see photo 2). Roll toward the centre, leaving about 1 inch (2.5cm) unrolled at the top (see photo 3).

Moisten the right-hand corner with water. Lap the right-hand corner over the left-hand corner, pressing together to seal (see photo 4). Repeat with remaining wrappers and filling.

In a large saucepan or covered casserole bring 64 fluid ounces (1.8l) *water* to the boil. Add *half* of the wontons, 1 at a time, to water. Return to the boil; reduce heat. Cover; simmer for 5 to 6 minutes or until pork in filling is no longer pink. Remove wontons and divide among 12 soup bowls. Repeat with remaining wontons. Meanwhile, in another large saucepan or covered casserole bring broth, rice wine or dry sherry, soy sauce, and sesame oil, if desired, to boiling point. Add spinach. Cook for 1 minute or just until spinach is limp. Ladle over wontons. If desired, sprinkle with thinly sliced spring onions. Makes 12 appetizer servings.

Pork and Prawn Filling: Use 4 ounces (110g) fresh *or* frozen shelled *prawns* (see tip, page 21) *or* 4½ ounces (125g) tinned *prawns,* drained. Thaw prawns, if frozen; chop finely. Mix 2 ounces (50g) finely chopped *water chestnuts;* 2 tablespoons finely chopped *spring onion;* 2 tablespoons *cornflour;* 1 tablespoon *rice wine or dry sherry;* 1 tablespoon *soy sauce;* 2 teaspoons grated *root ginger;** 1 teaspoon *sesame oil,* if desired; and ¼ teaspoon *pepper.* Add prawns and 4 ounces minced *pork;* mix well. Makes about 11 ounces (300g).

1 Spoon the filling just off-centre of the wonton or quartered egg roll wrapper. Measure the filling carefully; too much filling will make the wrapper difficult to seal.

See cutting technique, page 27.

2 Use your fingers to lift the point or corner of the wrapper nearest the filling. Fold the point over the filling, gently tucking it under the filling mixture to begin the roll.

Deep-Fried Wontons

Pork and Prawn Filling (see recipe, opposite), Date Filling, or Peanut Butter Filling
40 wonton wrappers or 10 egg roll wrappers, cut into quarters
Cooking oil for deep-fat frying
Sweet and Sour Sauce (see recipe, page 99) or icing sugar (optional)

Prepare desired filling. To make wontons, place 1 wonton or egg roll wrapper with 1 point toward you. Top with 1 rounded teaspoon of the filling just off-centre (see photo 1). Fold the nearest point of wrapper over filling, tucking the point under filling (see photo 2). Roll toward the centre, leaving about 1 inch (2.5cm) unrolled at the top (see photo 3).

Moisten the right-hand corner with water. Lap the right-hand corner over the left-hand corner, pressing together to seal (see photo 4). Repeat with remaining wrappers and filling.

In a wok, deep-fat fryer, or medium saucepan, heat 1½ to 2 inches (4 to 5 cm) cooking oil to 365°F (185°C) (see photo 1, page 82). Fry wontons, a few at a time, for 1½ to 2½ minutes or until golden brown, turning once. Remove wontons from oil and drain (see photo 4, page 83). Keep warm in a 300°F (150°C) gas mark 2 oven while frying remaining wontons. If desired, serve pork-and-prawn-filled wontons with Sweet and Sour Sauce. Or, sprinkle sweet-filled wontons with icing sugar. Makes 40.

Date Filling: In a small saucepan combine 8 ounces (225g) pitted whole *dates,* finely snipped; 2 ounces (50g) *caster sugar;* and 2 fluid ounces (55ml) *water.* Bring to the boil. Reduce heat to low. Cook, uncovered, about 4 minutes or until thickened, stirring constantly. Remove from heat. Stir in 2½ ounces (60g) finely chopped *walnuts,* ½ teaspoon finely grated *lemon peel,* 2 tablespoons *lemon juice,* and ½ teaspoon ground *cinnamon.* Cool. Makes about 14 ounces (400g).

Peanut Butter Filling: In a small mixing bowl stir together 8 ounces (225g) *peanut butter* and 2 ounces (50g) *soft brown sugar.* Stir in 1 ounce (25g) *desiccated coconut,* 2 tablespoons *Toasted Sesame Seed* (see recipe, page 10), and 2 teaspoons finely grated *orange peel.* Makes 12 ounces (350g).

3 Roll the wrapper and filling together toward the centre, stopping about 1 inch (2.5cm) from the point or corner opposite the roll. Avoid flattening the filling mixture as you roll.

4 Lap the moistened right-hand corner or point over the left-hand corner, pressing the ends together to seal. Moistening the wrapper with water helps seal the overlapped ends.

Crispy Spring Rolls

Deep-fried to a crisp and golden turn, spring rolls resemble egg rolls. The difference is in the wrapper. Our favourite comes from Vietnam. Made with tissue-thin rice papers, these light and crunchy rolls are eaten with fresh herbs, vegetables, and a dipping sauce.

Vietnamese Spring Rolls

Vietnamese Spring Rolls

Carrot Salad (optional) (**see recipe,** page 112)

Nuoc Cham (optional) (**see recipe,** page 40)

4 dried mushrooms
1 ounce (25g) bean threads
1 tablespoon cooking oil
2 cloves garlic, minced*
4 ounces (110g) minced pork
6 spring onions, thinly sliced
2 teaspoons fish sauce
1 teaspoon caster sugar
¼ teaspoon pepper
6 ounces (175g) tinned crabmeat, drained, flaked, and cartilage removed
1 medium carrot, grated
10 dried rice papers, *each* about 8 inches (20cm) in diameter
1 beaten egg
Cooking oil for deep-fat frying
Cucumber, sliced and cut into strips (optional)
Fresh mint (optional)
Fresh cilantro *or* parsley (optional)
Lettuce leaves (optional)

If desired, prepare Carrot Salad and Nuoc Cham; set aside. In a mixing bowl soak mushrooms in enough hot water to cover for 30 minutes. Rinse and squeeze to drain thoroughly. Chop finely, discarding stems. Meanwhile, in another bowl soak bean threads in enough hot water to cover for 30 minutes. Drain well; squeeze out excess moisture. Cut into 1-inch (2.5cm) lengths (see photo 1, page 18).

(See stir-frying photos, pages 24–25.) For filling, preheat a wok or large frying pan over high heat; add 1 tablespoon cooking oil. Stir-fry garlic for 15 seconds. Crumble pork into the wok. Stir-fry for 2 to 3 minutes or until no pink remains; drain off fat. Add spring onions, fish sauce, sugar, and pepper; stir-fry for 1 minute. Remove from heat. Stir in crabmeat, grated carrot, mushrooms, and bean threads; cool.

In a shallow dish, dip rice papers, 2 or 3 at a time, into warm water (see photo 1). Remove and place in a single layer on greaseproof paper; let stand for 2 minutes. Brush any dry edges with a little additional water; cover.

Cut *1* of the rice papers into quarters (see photo 2). On *each* quarter, spoon *1 tablespoon* of the filling along the curved edge (see photo 3). Fold curved edge over filling. Fold side corners toward the centre and roll up (see photo 4). Repeat with remaining papers and filling. Combine egg and 1 tablespoon *water.* Brush egg mixture over rolls.

In a wok, deep-fat fryer, or medium saucepan, heat 1½ to 2 inches (4 to 5cm) cooking oil to 365°F (185°C) (see photo 1, page 82). Fry spring rolls, 4 or 5 at a time, about 3 minutes or until light brown, turning once. Keep rolls separated when frying. Remove from oil and drain (see photo 4, page 83). Keep warm in a 300°F (150°C) gas mark 2 oven while frying remaining spring rolls.

To serve, let each person place a little Carrot Salad, cucumber, mint, and cilantro or parsley on a lettuce leaf, if desired. Add a spring roll; roll up. If desired, dip into Nuoc Cham before eating. Makes 40.

*See cutting technique, page 27.

1 To make the rice papers pliable, dip them into warm water in a shallow dish, such as a large pie tin.

2 Use a large sharp knife to cut the softened round rice paper into quarters, making pie-shaped wedges. Keep the remaining papers covered.

3 Spoon 1 tablespoon of the filling along the curved edge. Fold curved edge over filling.

4 To seal, fold the side corners of the rice paper toward the centre and over the filling. Then, roll the filling and the paper together.

House-to-House Dim Sum Party

Dining on dim sum—sweet and savoury Chinese snacks, dumplings, breads, even noodles—is a treat usually reserved for restaurants.

The variety of dishes makes a dim sum party at home a bit overwhelming, even for an experienced cook. But we've put together a dinner where each course is cooked and eaten at a different friend's house. That way, everyone shares in the cooking, the nibbling, and the fun.

Four-Flavoured Dumplings

Four-Flavoured Dumplings

Check the timetable on page 98 for our make-ahead suggestions for these eye-catching morsels.

3 dried mushrooms
 Dumpling Dough (see recipe, right)
 Pork and Prawn Filling (see recipe, page 88)
 Chilli Oil Dipping Sauce (optional) (see recipe, page 100)
1 ounce (25g) finely chopped fully cooked ham
1 ounce (25g) finely chopped carrot
2 spring onions, finely chopped

In a small mixing bowl soak mushrooms in enough hot water to cover for 30 minutes. Rinse; squeeze to drain thoroughly. Chop finely, discarding stems. Prepare Dumpling Dough.

Meanwhile, prepare Pork and Prawn Filling; set *half* of the filling aside. Wrap, seal, label, and freeze remaining filling for later use. Prepare Chilli Oil Dipping Sauce, if desired; set aside.

Divide dough in half. On a lightly floured surface roll *each* half to ¹⁄₁₆-inch (1.5mm) thickness. Using a biscuit cutter, cut into 3-inch (7.5cm) rounds, making a total of 30. (Reroll dough as needed.) Spoon *1 slightly rounded teaspoon* of the filling in the centre of *each* round (see photo 1).

For *each* dumpling, bring 2 opposite sides of round up over filling; pinch together *only* in the centre (see photo 2). Pinch together the remaining opposite sides *only* in the centre. Repeat with remaining rounds. Enlarge the openings atop dumplings (see photo 3). Place on a floured baking tray; cover. Chill dumplings in the freezer for 20 minutes.

Remove from the freezer; fill the openings atop dumplings with garnishes, using mushrooms, ham, carrot, and spring onion (see photo 4).

In a steamer place a greased steamer rack over water (see photo 2, page 70). Bring water to boiling over high heat. Place *half* of the dumplings on the rack so the sides do not touch (see photo 3, page 70). Cover and steam about 15 minutes or until pork is no longer pink. Remove and keep warm in a 300°F (150°C) gas mark 2 oven while steaming remaining dumplings. Serve with Chilli Oil Dipping Sauce, if desired. Makes 30.

Dumpling Dough

10 ounces (275g) plain flour
¼ teaspoon salt
5 fluid ounces (140ml) boiling water
2 fluid ounces (55ml) cold water
2 to 3 tablespoons plain flour

In a medium mixing bowl combine 10 ounces (275g) flour and salt. Gradually stir in boiling water, stirring constantly. Stir until combined. Stir in cold water. Turn out onto a lightly floured surface; let stand until cool enough to handle.

Knead in enough of the remaining 2 to 3 tablespoons flour to make a moderately stiff dough that is smooth and elastic (6 to 8 minutes). Shape into a ball; cover and let rest for 20 minutes. Use as directed in recipe.

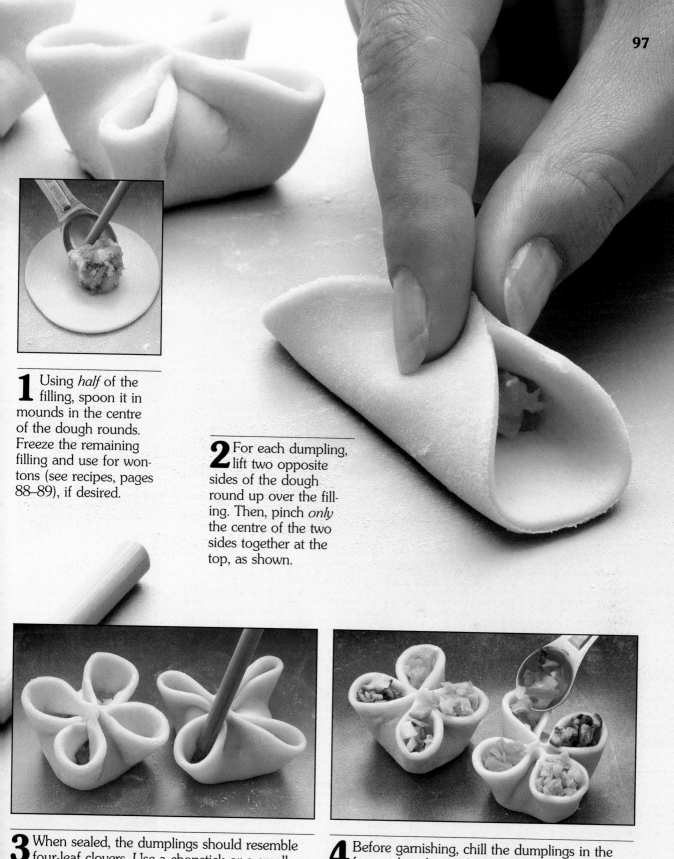

1 Using *half* of the filling, spoon it in mounds in the centre of the dough rounds. Freeze the remaining filling and use for wontons (see recipes, pages 88–89), if desired.

2 For each dumpling, lift two opposite sides of the dough round up over the filling. Then, pinch *only* the centre of the two sides together at the top, as shown.

3 When sealed, the dumplings should resemble four-leaf clovers. Use a chopstick or a small pointed spoon to enlarge the four openings atop each dumpling, as shown.

4 Before garnishing, chill the dumplings in the freezer, but do not freeze. Then, use a spoon to place the finely chopped garnishes in the openings, as shown.

Timetable

1st house
Four-Flavoured Dumplings.
- A few days before the party, shape and garnish dumplings, as shown. Steam, then cool. Seal, label, and freeze. (*Or, freeze before steaming.*)
- One hour before the party, prepare sauce.
- About 30 minutes before serving, reheat cooked frozen dumplings in a steamer for 10 to 15 minutes or till heated through. (*Or,* steam uncooked frozen dumplings as directed in the recipe.) Serve with a selection of beverages.

2nd house
Chinese Egg Rolls.
- Three hours before going to the first house, prepare egg rolls, *except do not deep-fry.* Prepare sauces. Cover and chill egg rolls and sauces.
- About 20 minutes before serving, deep-fry egg rolls and reheat Sweet and Sour Sauce. Serve with a selection of beverages.

3rd house
Potstickers.
- A few days before the party, prepare Potstickers, *except do not cook.* Seal, label, and freeze.
- One hour before going to the first house, prepare dipping sauces.
- About 20 minutes before serving, cook frozen Potstickers in a frying pan, as shown. Serve with a selection of beverages.

4th house
Skewered Pork.
- Three to four hours before going to the first house, marinate pork. Then, thread pork on the skewers. Cover and chill.
- About 10 minutes before serving, grill pork. Arrange on a serving dish. Serve with a selection of beverages.

5th house
Chinese Buns.
- Three hours before going to the first house, prepare buns, *except do not steam.* Cover buns and chill.
- About 20 minutes before serving, steam buns. Serve with a selection of beverages.

Chinese Egg Rolls

Fill the egg rolls before the party, then chill. Deep-fry just before serving.

8 dried mushrooms
1 whole medium chicken breast
    (about 12 ounces [350g]), skinned
    and boned (see tip, page 34)
1 tablespoon rice wine *or* dry sherry
1 tablespoon cooking oil
2 teaspoons grated root ginger*
8 ounces (225g) fresh bean sprouts
2 medium carrots, grated
4 spring onions, thinly sliced
1 teaspoon caster sugar
1 teaspoon sesame oil (optional)
¼ teaspoon salt
    Sweet and Sour Sauce (optional)
    (see recipe, right)
    Hot Mustard Sauce (optional)
    (see recipe, page 10)
10 egg roll wrappers
    Cooking oil for deep-fat frying

In a small mixing bowl soak mushrooms in enough hot water to cover for 30 minutes. Rinse well and squeeze to drain thoroughly. Chop finely, discarding stems.

Cut chicken into thin strips; cut strips into matchstick-size shreds. In a mixing bowl sprinkle rice wine or dry sherry over chicken.

(See stir-frying photos, pages 24–25 and 30–31.) For filling, preheat a wok or large frying pan over high heat; add 1 tablespoon cooking oil. (Add more oil as necessary during cooking.) Stir-fry root ginger in hot oil for 15 seconds. Add chicken; stir-fry for 1½ minutes. Add bean sprouts, carrots, spring onions, and mushrooms. Stir-fry for 2 minutes or until chicken is done and vegetables are crisp-tender. Stir in sugar; sesame oil, if desired; and salt. Remove filling mixture from heat; cool.

Meanwhile, if desired, prepare Sweet and Sour Sauce and Hot Mustard Sauce. To make rolls, place *1* egg roll wrapper with 1 point toward

you. Spoon *about 2* ounces (50g) of the cool filling diagonally just off-centre of wrapper (see photo 1, page 88). Fold the nearest point of wrapper over filling, tucking the point under filling (see photo 2, page 88). Fold the side corners toward the centre and roll up (see photo 4, page 93). Moisten the top point with water; press on roll to seal. Repeat with remaining egg roll wrappers and filling mixture.

In a wok, deep-fat fryer, or medium saucepan, heat 1½ to 2 inches (4 to 5cm) of cooking oil to 365°F (185°C) (see photo 1, page 82). Fry egg rolls, 2 or 3 at a time, for 2 to 4 minutes or until golden brown, turning once. Remove from oil and drain (see photo 4, page 83). Keep warm in a 300°F (150°C) gas mark 2 oven while frying remaining egg rolls. To serve, cut into thirds. Serve with sauces, if desired. Makes 10.

Sweet and Sour Sauce

6 fluid ounces (165ml) orange juice
1½ ounces (40g) soft brown sugar
3 tablespoons rice vinegar *or* vinegar
1 tablespoon cornflour
2 teaspoons soy sauce

In a small saucepan stir together orange juice, soft brown sugar, rice vinegar or vinegar, cornflour, and soy sauce. Cook and stir over medium heat until thickened and bubbly; cook and stir 2 minutes more. Serve warm or at room temperature. Makes about 8 fluid ounces (220ml).

Microwave Directions: In a 16-fluid-ounce (440ml) glass measure combine orange juice, soft brown sugar, rice vinegar or vinegar, cornflour, and soy sauce. Micro-cook mixture, uncovered, on 100% power (HIGH) for 2½ to 3½ minutes or until thickened and bubbly, stirring every minute until slightly thickened, then every 30 seconds. Cook, on high 30 seconds more. Serve warm or at room temperature.

*See cutting technique, page 27.

Potstickers

Dumpling Dough (see recipe, page 96)
1   **tablespoon cornflour**
1   **tablespoon soy sauce**
1   **teaspoon grated root ginger***
1   **teaspoon sesame oil (optional)**
½   **teaspoon caster sugar**
1   **clove garlic, minced***
8   **ounces (225g) minced pork**
5   **ounces (150g) finely chopped
     Chinese cabbage**
1   **spring onion, finely chopped
     Soy-Vinegar Sauce (see recipe, page
     53) or Chilli Oil Dipping Sauce
     (optional)
     Cooking oil**

Prepare dough. For filling, mix cornflour; soy sauce; root ginger; sesame oil, if desired; sugar; and garlic. Add pork, cabbage, and onion; mix well. Set aside. Prepare sauce, if desired.

Divide dough in half. On a lightly floured surface roll *each* half to slightly less than ⅛-inch (3mm) thickness. Using a biscuit cutter, cut into 3½-inch (8.5cm) rounds, making a total of 30. (Reroll dough as needed.) Spoon *about 2 teaspoons* of the filling in the centre of *each* round. For *each* dumpling, moisten the edge of the round with water. Fold round in half. Fold small pleats *only* along 1 edge, pressing pleats against the other edge to seal. Place, pleated side up, on a floured baking tray; cover.

In a 12-inch (30cm) frying pan heat *2 tablespoons* cooking oil over medium-high heat for 1 minute. Arrange *half* of the dumplings in the frying pan, pleated side up. Cook, uncovered, for 1 to 2 minutes or until the bottoms are light brown. Reduce heat to low. Remove from heat; add 5 fluid ounces (140ml) *water* all at once near the edge of the frying pan. Return to heat. Cover; cook for 10 minutes. Increase heat to medium-high. Uncover; cook for 3 to 5 minutes or until all water evaporates. Add *2 teaspoons* cooking oil. Tilt the frying pan to coat the bottom. Cook, uncovered, for 1 minute.

Remove dumplings; drain on kitchen paper. Keep warm in a 300°F (150°C) gas mark 2 oven while frying remaining dumplings. If desired, serve with dipping sauce. Makes 30.

Chilli Oil Dipping Sauce: Mix 3 fluid ounces (80ml) *white rice vinegar, red rice vinegar, or vinegar;* 2 fluid ounces (55ml) *soy sauce;* and 1 to 2 teaspoons *chilli oil or Chilli Oil* (see tip, page 11). Makes about 5 fluid ounces (140ml).

Skewered Pork

12   **ounces (350g) tenderloin of pork**
2   **fluid ounces (55ml) hoisin sauce**
2   **fluid ounces (55ml) rice wine or
     dry sherry**
2   **tablespoons soy sauce**
1   **tablespoon sesame oil or cooking oil**
1   **teaspoon caster sugar**
1   **teaspoon grated root ginger**
1   **clove garlic, minced**
8   **spring onions, bias-sliced into 1½-inch
     (4cm) pieces**

Soak ten 9- to 10-inch (23 to 25.5cm) bamboo skewers in hot water for 30 minutes. (Or, use metal skewers and omit soaking.) Cut pork diagonally into ¼-inch (.5cm)-thick strips; place in shallow baking dish. For marinade, mix hoisin sauce, rice wine or dry sherry, soy sauce, sesame oil or cooking oil, sugar, root ginger, and garlic; pour over pork. Cover; let stand at room temperature for 30 minutes, stirring occasionally.

Drain pork, reserving marinade. Thread pork and onions on the skewers, allowing a ¼-inch (.5cm) space between pieces (see photo 1, page 65). Preheat the grill. Place skewers on the unheated rack of a grill pan. Broil 4 to 5 inches (10 to 13cm) from heat for 7 to 9 minutes or until no pink remains in the pork, turning once and brushing often with reserved marinade (see photo 3, page 65). If desired, garnish with *kiwi fruit, pineapple,* and fresh *cilantro or parsley.* Makes 10 appetizer servings.

See cutting technique, page 27.

Chinese Buns

You'll need a large layered steamer to steam all the buns at once. Or, improvise with two or more smaller steamers (see tip, page 74).

1 **pound to 1 pound plus 3 ounces (450g to 525g) plain flour**
1 **packet dried yeast****
8 **fluid ounces (220ml) milk**
2 **tablespoons caster sugar**
1 **tablespoon lard**
½ **teaspoon salt**
2 **egg whites**
   Pork Filling *or* Sweet Bean-Date Filling

For dough, in a mixing bowl combine *7½ ounces (210g)* of the flour and yeast. In a small saucepan heat milk, sugar, lard, and salt just warm (115°F or 46°C) and lard is almost melted, stirring constantly. Add to flour mixture; add egg whites. Beat with an electric mixer on low speed for 30 seconds, scraping the bowl constantly. Beat on high speed for 3 minutes. Using a spoon, stir in as much of the remaining flour as you can.

On a lightly floured surface knead in enough of the remaining flour to make a moderately stiff dough that is smooth and elastic (6 to 8 minutes). Shape into a ball. Place in a greased bowl; turn once to grease surface. Cover and let rise in a warm place until double (about 1 hour). Meanwhile, prepare desired filling.

To shape buns, punch dough down; divide into 20 balls. Cover and let rest for 10 minutes. Flatten *each* ball into a 3½-inch (8.5cm) circle. For *each* bun, place *2 scant tablespoons* of the pork filling or *1 scant tablespoon* of the sweet filling in the centre of the circle. Bring up edges; moisten and press to seal seams. Place, seam side down, on a lightly greased baking tray. Repeat with remaining circles and filling. If desired, dip a small Oriental rubber stamp or the square end of a chopstick into red food colouring; press atop sweet-filled buns *only*. Cover; let rise in a warm place for 20 minutes. (*Or*, if buns are not steamed immediately after rising, omit rising. After shaping, cover; chill for up to 6 hours.)

In a layered steamer place a greased steamer rack over water (see photo 2, page 70). Bring water to the boil over high heat. Place buns on the racks so the sides do not touch (see photo 3, page 70). Cover; steam about 15 minutes or until buns spring back when touched. Serve buns warm. Makes 20.

Pork Filling: In a small mixing bowl soak 12 dried *mushrooms* in enough hot water to cover for 30 minutes. Rinse and squeeze to drain thoroughly. Chop finely, discarding stems. Meanwhile, in a medium mixing bowl toss together 12 ounces (350g) lean boneless *pork*, diced; 2 teaspoons *caster sugar;* 2 teaspoons *soy sauce;* and ¼ teaspoon *pepper.* For sauce, in another small mixing bowl mix 3 tablespoons *oyster sauce,* 2 tablespoons *water,* and 1½ teaspoons *cornflour;* set aside.

(See stir-frying photos, pages 24–25 and 30–31.) Preheat a wok or large frying pan over high heat; add 1 tablespoon *cooking oil.* (Add more oil as necessary during cooking.) Stir-fry 2 teaspoons grated *root ginger** in hot oil for 15 seconds. Add 3 thinly sliced *spring onions;* stir-fry for 1 minute. Add pork; stir-fry for 2 to 3 minutes or until no pink remains in pork. Push from the centre of the wok.

Stir sauce; add to the centre of the wok or frying pan. Cook and stir until thickened and bubbly; cook and stir for 2 minutes more. Stir in mushrooms and 4 ounces (110g) *bamboo shoots,* drained and chopped; remove from heat. Makes about 14 ounces (400g).

Sweet Bean-Date Filling: In a small mixing bowl combine 6 ounces (175g) tinned *sweet red bean paste,* 1½ ounces (40g) finely snipped stoned *dates,* 2½ ounces (60g) finely chopped *walnuts,* and 1 or 2 drops *vanilla essence.* Makes about 10 ounces (275g).

**Note: Quick-rising active dried yeast is not recommended in this recipe.

Szechwan Duck

The contrast of crisp and
tender is nowhere more
delightful than in this
Szechwan dish. The secret
of this specialty? A pairing
of cooking methods.

First the duck is gently
steamed. Then it is deep-
fried to seal in the juices
and to crisp the skin. The
result: an extraordinary
blend of textures you'll
savour with every bite.

Crispy Szechwan Duck

Crispy Szechwan Duck

1 **4- to 5-pound (1kg800g to 2kg250g) duckling**
2 **tablespoons whole Szechwan peppers or whole black peppers**
2 **star anise or 2 teaspoons aniseed**
3 **spring onions, thinly sliced**
2 **tablespoons rice wine or dry sherry**
1 **tablespoon grated root ginger***
1 **teaspoon salt**
Lotus Leaf Buns (see recipe, page 74)
2 **tablespoons soy sauce**
2 **teaspoons five-spice powder or Five-Spice Powder (see tip, page 11)**
2 **ounces (50g) cornflour**
Cooking oil for deep-fat frying
Hoisin sauce or sweet bean sauce
Spring onion slivers*

Rinse duck; pat dry. Place duck, breast side up, on a counter surface. Press down firmly on the breastbone to flatten (see photo 1).

Using a mortar and pestle or a rolling pin, crush Szechwan or black peppers and star anise or aniseed; strain, if desired. In a small mixing bowl combine pepper mixture, sliced spring onions, rice wine or dry sherry, root ginger, and salt. Rub mixture over duck and inside cavity. Cover and chill for 6 hours or overnight.

In a steamer place a greased steamer rack over water (see photo 2, page 70). Bring water to the boil over high heat. Place seasoned duck, breast side up, on the rack (see photo 3, page 70). Cover; steam for 2 hours. (Add boiling water as needed.) Prepare Lotus Leaf Buns.

Remove duck from the steamer; discard cooking juices. Using kitchen paper, wipe duck to remove onion mixture. Let duck stand, uncovered, at room temperature, for 30 minutes.

In a small mixing bowl combine soy sauce and five-spice powder. Brush over duck. Sprinkle cornflour on duck, pressing lightly with fingers, to coat evenly. Let stand for 15 minutes.

Meanwhile, in a large wok or a large covered casserole heat 1½ inches (4cm) cooking oil to 375°F (190°C) (see photo 1, page 82). Using 2 large long-handled spoons, *carefully* lower duck, breast side up, into hot oil (see photo 2). Fry duck for 8 to 10 minutes or until crisp and golden brown on the bottom, occasionally spooning hot oil over duck. Use spoons to prevent duck from sticking to the sides of the wok.

Carefully turn duck. Fry for 8 to 10 minutes more or until crisp and golden brown, moving duck to prevent sticking. Remove from oil and drain on kitchen paper.

If desired, carve duck Oriental style (see tip, opposite). Serve with buns, hoisin or sweet bean sauce, and spring onion slivers. To eat, open bun; spread with a little sauce. Add a few onion slivers and some duck. Eat as a sandwich. Makes 5 servings.

1 Using both hands, press down firmly on the breast side of the duck to flatten the breastbone. This makes the duck easier to handle when it is deep-fat fried in the wok.

2 Insert a long-handled spoon into the tail end of the duck. Use another spoon under the opposite end to slowly lower the duck into the hot oil, as shown. (Be sure the deep-fat frying thermometer is secure.)

*See cutting technique, page 27.

Oriental-Style Carving

1 Use a cleaver to remove the wings and legs of the duck. Then, with one hand, stand the duck, tail side up. Use kitchen paper to protect your hand from the heat. Halve the duck lengthwise between the breast and the back, as shown.

2 Use kitchen shears to cut along the backbone. Discard the backbone and the tail. Chop the back sections into 1- to 1½-inch (2.5 to 4cm) pieces, cutting through the meat and bone. Reassemble the back, skin side down, on a serving dish.

3 Use a boning knife to remove the meat, in one piece, from the breast-bone. Discard the collarbone. Halve the breast lengthwise, then crosswise into 1- to 1½-inch (2.5 to 4cm) pieces. Reassemble the breast meat, skin side up, atop the back.

4 Use a cleaver to separate the legs from the thighs. Then, chop each wing, leg, and thigh into two sections, cutting through the meat and bone, as shown. Arrange the wings, legs, and thighs in their original shape on the dish.

Oriental Dinner Party

You love Oriental food but think it's too much work for entertaining? It doesn't have to be if you follow our lead. We've organized the menu and preplanned the cooking, and we take you step by step through the timetable. After your guests depart, you'll wonder why you waited so long to "go Oriental."

Menu

- Oriental Cold Plate*

- Moo Shu Pork with Mandarin Pancakes*

- Marinated Salmon*

- Mange Tout with Corn*

- Hot cooked rice

- Fruit Platter*

See pages 108-113

*Moo Shu Pork with
Mandarin Pancakes*

Moo Shu Pork with Mandarin Pancakes

Mandarin Pancakes
  8 **ounces (225g) boneless pork**
  2 **teaspoons soy sauce**
  1 **teaspoon rice wine *or* dry sherry**
  4 **dried mushrooms**
  1 **dried cloud ear**
  ½ **ounce (10g) dried lily buds**
     Spring Onion Brushes
        (see tip, page 71)
  2 **tablespoons cooking oil**
  2 **beaten eggs**
  2 **teaspoons grated root ginger***
  1 **small carrot, cut into julienne strips***
  3 **spring onions, cut into 1½-inch (4cm)**
        slivers*
  3 **ounces (75g) shredded Chinese**
        cabbage
  1 **tablespoon soy sauce**
  ½ **teaspoon sesame oil (optional)**
  ¼ **teaspoon caster sugar**
     Hoisin sauce

Prepare Mandarin Pancakes. Partially freeze pork; thinly slice across the grain into strips. Cut strips into matchstick-size shreds (*see* tip, page 35). For marinade, in a medium mixing bowl mix 2 teaspoons soy sauce and rice wine or dry sherry; stir in pork. Cover; let stand at room temperature for 30 minutes. Stir occasionally. (*Or,* marinate in the refrigerator for 2 hours.)

In another mixing bowl soak mushrooms, cloud ear, and lily buds in enough hot water to cover for 30 minutes. Rinse and squeeze to drain thoroughly. Cut mushrooms and cloud ear into julienne strips*, discarding stems. Cut lily buds into 1-inch (2.5cm) pieces. Prepare Spring Onion Brushes, cutting *only* 1 end of *each* onion.

Preheat a wok or large frying pan over medium heat; add *1 tablespoon* of the cooking oil. Add eggs; lift and tilt the wok or frying pan to form a thin "egg sheet" (*see* photo 3, page 39). Cook, without stirring, about 2 minutes or just until set.

Slide egg sheet onto a cutting board. Thinly slice into bite-size strips; set aside.

(See stir-frying photos, pages 24–25 and 30–31.) Return the wok or frying pan to high heat. Add remaining cooking oil to the hot wok. (Add more cooking oil as necessary during cooking.) Stir-fry root ginger for 15 seconds. Add carrot; stir-fry for 1½ minutes. Add *half* of the spring onion slivers and cabbage; stir-fry for 1½ minutes. Remove vegetables.

Add pork mixture to the hot wok or frying pan. Stir-fry for 2 to 3 minutes or until no pink remains. Return vegetables to wok. Add mushrooms; cloud ear; lily buds; 1 tablespoon soy sauce; sesame oil, if desired; and sugar. Stir for 1 minute or until heated through. Stir in egg strips.

To serve, let each person brush a little hoisin sauce on a pancake, using an onion brush (*see* photo, page 107). Spoon *about 1½ ounces (40g)* of the pork mixture in the centre of pancake; top with a few remaining spring onion slivers. Fold filling and pancake envelope-style or Swiss-roll style (*see* photo 4). Eat out of hand. Makes 8 servings.

Mandarin Pancakes: Prepare ½ of the recipe for Dumpling Dough (*see* recipe, page 96). On a lightly floured surface form dough into an 8-inch (20cm)-long roll. Cut into 1-inch (2.5cm) pieces. Flatten *each* piece into a 3-inch (7.5cm) round (*see* photo 1). To make pancakes, roll *each* round into a 6-inch (15cm) circle. Lightly brush one side of *each* circle with *cooking oil or sesame oil (see* photo 2). Make stacks of 2 pancakes each, oiled sides together; cover. Heat a heavy ungreased frying pan or griddle over medium-high heat. Add 1 pancake stack. Cook for 30 seconds to 1 minute on *each* side or until bubbles appear on the surface and the bottom begins to brown. Remove from the frying pan. Separate pancakes (*see* photo 3). Cover. Repeat, cooking remaining stacks. Makes 8.

*See cutting technique, page 27.

1 Use the tips of your fingers to gently flatten each piece of dumpling dough into a 3-inch (7.5cm) round. Work quickly to prevent the dough from drying out.

2 Brush a little cooking oil or sesame oil on one side of *each* circle. This keeps the pancakes from sticking together when they are stacked for cooking.

3 Because the pancakes are fragile, cook them in stacks of two each. Then, gently separate the cooked pancakes, using your fingers, as shown.

4 To fold the filling and pancake envelope style, bring one edge of the pancake up to overlap the filling. Then, lap the two adjacent edges of the pancake over the filling (as shown, front). Or, roll the filling and pancake together Swiss-roll style (as shown, back).

Timetable

3 or 4 days before
- Make Mandarin Pancakes. After cooking, separate pancakes, as shown. Then, cool, seal, label, and freeze pancakes.
- Prepare Kimchi. Cover and let stand in a cool place (60°F or 15°C) for 3 days. Then, store in the refrigerator.

1 day before
- Grate carrot for Carrot Salad, as shown. Marinate in the refrigerator. Prepare Red-Cooked Beef and Asparagus in Miso. Cover and chill.

6 hrs. before
- Remove pancakes from the freezer to thaw.
- Marinate salmon in the refrigerator.
- Prepare fruit and arrange Fruit Platter. Cover and chill till serving time.
- Set the table. Arrange a serving area for guests to help themselves to Oriental Cold Plate and Moo Shu Pork with Mandarin Pancakes.

2 hrs. before
- Prepare ingredients for Moo Shu Pork and Mange Tout with Corn.
- Arrange foods for Oriental Cold Plate on a large serving dish. Cover and chill. Remove from the refrigerator about 30 minutes before guests arrive.
- Measure rice and start cooking it about 30 minutes before serving the main course.

Before Serving
- Reheat pancakes in a steamer or in the oven.
- To reheat in a steamer, wrap pancakes in a cloth napkin and steam for 5 minutes. Or, layer pancakes with foil on a foil-lined baking tray. Cover and heat in a 375°F (190°C) gas mark 5 oven about 7 minutes.
- Stir-fry Moo Shu Pork.
- Offer sake or Chinese beer with appetizers.
- Make tea.
- Place salmon in the oven. Prepare mange tout.
- Arrange food in serving dishes and pour tea.

Oriental Cold Plate

Before dinner, invite guests to sample this spicy assortment with Moo Shu Pork (see recipe, page 108).

Kimchi (see recipe, below)
Red-Cooked Beef (see recipe, right)
Asparagus in Miso (see recipe, page 112)
Carrot Salad (see recipe, page 112)
Lettuce leaves

Prepare Kimchi, Red-Cooked Beef, Asparagus in Miso, and Carrot Salad. To serve, line a large serving dish with lettuce leaves. Arrange desired amount of beef and vegetables over lettuce. Makes 8 appetizer servings.

Kimchi

1½ to 2 pounds (700 to 900g) Chinese cabbage *or* bok choy, cut into 1½-inch (4cm) pieces
32 fluid ounces (900ml) water
3 ounces (75g) salt
4 ounces (110g) daikon, peeled and cut into julienne strips*
3 spring onions, cut into slivers*
2 teaspoons salted shrimp *or* shrimp paste
2 cloves garlic, minced*
2 teaspoons caster sugar
1 teaspoon ground red pepper
1 teaspoon grated root ginger*

In a large mixing bowl combine cabbage or bok choy, water, and salt. Let stand for 4 hours. Drain; rinse well with cold water. Drain again.

In the same bowl combine daikon, spring onions, salted shrimp or shrimp paste, garlic, sugar, red pepper, and root ginger. Add cabbage; mix well. Press mixture into a small jar. Secure lid. Let stand in cool place (about 60°F or 15°C) for 3 days. Makes about 32 ounces (900g).

Red-Cooked Beef

Savour a sensational blend of spices in this cold meat dish from China.

2 tablespoons dried tangerine peel *or* Dried Tangerine Peel (see tip, page 11)
2 star anise *or* 2 teaspoons aniseed
2 teaspoons whole Szechwan peppers *or* whole black peppers
1 teaspoon cardamom seed
½ teaspoon fennel seed
2 whole cloves
16 fluid ounces (440ml) water
8 fluid ounces (220ml) soy sauce
2 ounces (50g) caster sugar
2 pounds (900g) silverside of beef

For spice bag, wrap tangerine peel, star anise or aniseed, Szechwan or black peppers, cardamom, fennel, and cloves in cheesecloth (see photo 1, page 14). In a large covered casserole combine water, soy sauce, sugar, and spice bag. Bring to the boil.

Trim excess fat from meat. Place meat in soy mixture. Return to boiling; reduce heat. Cover and simmer for 45 minutes.

Turn meat. Simmer, covered, for 45 to 55 minutes more or until meat is tender, basting often with cooking liquid during the last 10 minutes (see photo 2, page 14).

Remove meat from casserole, reserving cooking liquid. When cool enough to handle, cover meat and chill. Strain reserved liquid and discard spice bag (see photo 3, page 14). Skim fat from liquid. Store liquid in the refrigerator for up to 3 days or in the freezer for up to 6 months. Reuse for other red-cooked dishes or pass with cold meat, if desired.

To serve, cut meat across the grain into ⅛-inch (3mm)-thick slices. Serve as part of a cold plate or use in sandwiches. Makes 8 servings.

See cutting technique, page 27.

Carrot Salad

A popular accompaniment to many Vietnamese meals.

8 fluid ounces (220ml) water
3 tablespoons vinegar
2 tablespoons caster sugar
Dash salt
3 medium carrots, finely grated

In a medium mixing bowl combine water, vinegar, sugar, and salt; stir until sugar dissolves. Stir in grated carrots. Cover and marinate in the refrigerator overnight. Drain carrots before serving. Makes 14 ounces (400g).

Marinated Salmon

8 fresh *or* frozen salmon *or* other fish steaks (2 to 2½ pounds [900g to 1kg125g])
3 fluid ounces (80ml) sake *or* dry sherry
3 fluid ounces (80ml) mirin
2 fluid ounces (55ml) soy sauce
1 tablespoon cooking oil
1 tablespoon lemon juice
Lemon wedges *or* lemon slice twists (optional)
Fresh cilantro *or* parsley (optional)

Thaw fish, if frozen. Rinse and pat dry. For marinade, in a shallow dish combine sake or dry sherry, mirin, soy sauce, oil, and lemon juice. Add fish; cover and marinate in the refrigerator for 4 to 6 hours, turning steaks once.

Drain fish, reserving marinade. Measure thickness of fish. Place fish in a greased shallow baking tin. Bake, uncovered, in a 450°F (230°C) gas mark 8 oven until fish flakes easily with a fork. Allow 4 to 6 minutes for each ½ inch (1cm) of thickness. Brush with some of reserved marinade after 5 minutes. If desired, garnish with lemon and cilantro or parsley. Makes 8 servings.

Asparagus in Miso

Japanese miso adds a touch of sweetness and a creamy appearance to cold asparagus.

1½ pounds (700g) cut asparagus, fresh *or* frozen
2 fluid ounces (55ml) white miso
2 tablespoons sake *or* dry sherry
1 tablespoon water
1 teaspoon caster sugar
1 tablespoon Toasted Sesame Seed (see recipe, page 10)

If using fresh asparagus, wash and scrape off scales, if desired. Break off bases at the point where spears snap easily; discard bases. Bias-slice spears into 2-inch (5cm) pieces.* In a medium saucepan cook asparagus in a small amount of boiling water about 6 minutes or until crisp-tender. (Or, cook frozen asparagus according to packet directions, omitting salt.) Drain asparagus and set aside.

In a large mixing bowl combine white miso, sake or dry sherry, water, and sugar; mix well. Add asparagus; toss gently. Cover; marinate in the refrigerator for at least 2 hours or overnight. Let asparagus stand at room temperature for 30 minutes before serving; sprinkle with sesame seed. Makes about 1½ pounds (700g).

See cutting technique, page 27.

Mange Tout with Corn

12 ounces (350g) fresh *or* frozen mange
   tout, thawed
15 ounces (425g) tinned whole baby sweet
   corn, drained
 2 teaspoons cooking oil
 2 teaspoons grated root ginger*
 2 spring onions, thinly sliced
 1 teaspoon caster sugar
 ½ teaspoon sesame oil (optional)
 ¼ teaspoon salt

If using fresh mange tout, remove tips and strings; rinse and drain. Halve baby corn lengthwise, then crosswise; set aside.

(See stir-frying photos, pages 24–25.) Preheat a wok or large frying pan over high heat; add cooking oil. Stir-fry root ginger in hot oil for 15 seconds. Add spring onions; stir-fry for 1 minute. Add mange tout; stir-fry for 1 minute. Add corn; sugar; sesame oil, if desired; and salt. Cook and stir about 1 minute or until heated through. Makes 8 servings.

Fruit Platter

2½ pounds (1kg125g) assorted fresh fruit
   (sliced papaya, cubed mango, whole
   or sliced strawberries, sliced kiwi
   fruit, orange sections *and/or*
   pineapple wedges)
20 ounces (560g) tinned whole stoned
   lychees, drained
15 ounces (425g) tinned whole stoned
   loquats, drained

Arrange fresh fruit, lychees, and loquats on a large serving dish; cover and chill until serving time. Makes 8 servings.

Oriental Menu Planning

Once you've mastered the skills of Oriental cooking, you'll want to share your expertise with friends. But as with any dinner party, organizing an Oriental party menu requires a little planning and practice. Here are a few ideas to get you started.

● Select foods with eye and taste appeal. All dishes in the meal should complement one another.

● Plan a menu with familiar foods—ones you are comfortable serving. Then, add an Oriental recipe, such as a soup or a vegetable stir-fry. As you gain confidence, increase the number of Oriental foods on the menu. And don't forget to serve plenty of rice, the mainstay of most Oriental meals.

● As you add more Oriental dishes to the menu, include some that can be made ahead. Avoid serving more than one or two stir-frys that require last-minute cooking.

● Set the table with rice bowls, tea cups, dinner plates, soup spoons, and chopsticks or forks.

● Place all the food on the table at the same time, including the soup.

● Skip the dessert or offer a selection of fresh fruit. In Oriental countries, sweets are usually reserved for banquets or snacks.

Oriental Ingredients

Need help selecting Oriental ingredients? Then you've turned to the right pages. Whether you need lemongrass, fish sauce, or udon, you'll find these next few pages valuable.

Look for these products in the Oriental section at your supermarket, or visit an Oriental grocer. If you can't find an ingredient, use our suggested substitute. Or, if it's a seasoning, simply omit the item from the recipe. Although the flavour will be changed somewhat, you still will enjoy the dish.

Cereal and Bean Products

Bean Threads (4)
Also called cellophane noodles, bean threads are made from ground mung beans. Soften in hot water before using.

Buckwheat Noodles (10)
Known as soba in Japan, these thin dried noodles are made from buckwheat flour. Substitute dried fine egg noodles, if desired.

Egg Noodles, Chinese (1)
Made from wheat flour, water, and egg, Chinese noodles are sold fresh or dried. Substitute American-made or Italian fine egg noodles.

Egg Roll Wrappers (15)
These thin square sheets of noodle dough are called egg roll wrappers or skins. Buy them fresh or frozen.

Fermented Bean Curd (17)
Sometimes called bean curd cheese, fermented bean curd is sold in two forms. The "white" is fermented with or without chilli, and the "red" is fermented with rice wine and salt.

Fermented Black Beans (13)
These soyabeans are cooked, fermented in a salt brine, then dried. Rinse and finely chop before using.

Hot Bean Paste (7)
A thick reddish sauce with a fiery flavour, hot bean paste combines soyabeans, chilli peppers, and spices.

Miso (8)
A fermented soyabean paste that includes other grains, miso is a Japanese product sold in many colours, textures, and flavours.

Potsticker Wrappers (14)
Made from flour and water, these round dumpling wrappers can be purchased or made at home.

Rice, Long Grain (3)
A staple in most Chinese diets, long grain rice is preferred by most Chinese cooks over the short grain varieties.

Rice Papers (11)
Thin and brittle, dried round rice papers are made from rice flour and used as a wrapper by Vietnamese cooks.

Rice, Short Grain (5)
A favourite of Japanese cooks, short grain rice is slightly sticky when it is cooked.

Rice Sticks (9)
Made from rice flour, rice sticks are also called rice noodles or rice vermicelli. Soften in hot water before using. Substitute cooked fine egg noodles, if desired.

Sweet Bean Sauce (6)
Made from fermented soyabeans, sweet bean sauce has a salty sweet flavour. Substitute hoisin sauce, if desired.

Tofu (16)
Soyabeans are used to make this custardlike high-protein food. Tofu is also called fresh bean curd or bean cake.

Udon (2)
Also known as white noodles, this thick, broad Japanese pasta is made from wheat flour. Buy it fresh or dried.

Wonton Wrappers (12)
Prepared from noodle dough, these wrappers or skins are sold fresh or frozen. Substitute egg roll wrappers, cut into quarters, if desired.

1

2

3

4

5

6

7

8

9

10

Fruits and Vegetables

Baby Sweet Corn (10)
Miniature in size, baby corn is 1½ to 2 inches (4 to 5cm) long. Buy it tinned.

Bamboo Shoots (17)
These ivory-coloured shoots come sliced or cone shaped. Buy the shoots tinned.

Bean Sprouts (19)
Grown from mung beans, fresh bean sprouts are white, with tiny caps and a crisp texture. Buy them fresh or tinned.

Bok Choy (15)
A Chinese cabbage with white stalks and dark green leaves, bok choy has a sweet flavour.

Chilli Peppers (21)
Asian chilli peppers are often unavailable. Substitute red or green chilli or jalapeño peppers. Always handle with gloved hands to protect skin from pepper oils.

Chinese Cabbage (11)
Sometimes called Napa or celery cabbage, this elongated cabbage has a mild sweet flavour and pale green wrinkled leaves.

Cilantro (9)
Also called fresh coriander or Chinese parsley, cilantro has a stronger flavour and fragrance than parsley.

Daikon (8)
This large sweet-tasting Japanese white radish may be long or round. Substitute turnip or white radish, if desired.

Enoki Mushrooms (20)
Also known as enokitake mushrooms, enoki are prized for their tiny caps, delicate flavour, and crisp texture.

Root Ginger (7)
Root ginger has a brown skin and a cream-coloured flesh, with a pungent flavour.

Kiwi Fruit (6)
Initially known as the Chinese gooseberry, kiwi fruit has a fuzzy brown skin and a tart-sweet green flesh with tiny black seeds. Peel before using.

Lemongrass (12)
Lemon-flavoured lemongrass resembles a fibrous spring onion. Buy it fresh or dried. Substitute lemon peel, if desired.

Lychee (3)
Also spelled litchi, this sweet juicy white fruit has a hard red shell. Lychees are most often sold tinned.

Loquat (4)
Orange-coloured fruit with a slightly tart flavour, loquats are available tinned or dried.

Mango (2)
Ripe mangoes vary in colour from green to yellow to red. They taste similar to apricots and have juicy flesh.

Oriental Chrysanthemum Leaves (18)
These fresh greens are called shungiku in Japan. *Do not* confuse them with the toxic common flowering plant. Discard the roots and flowering buds before using.

Papaya (5)
When ripe, this pear-shape fruit has yellowish skin and buttery-tasting golden flesh. Edible peppery black seeds fill the centre cavity.

Mange Tout (16)
Also known as sugar peas, snow peas, or pea pods, mange tout conceal flat tiny peas. They have a sweet flavour and crisp texture. Buy them fresh or frozen.

Pickled Ginger (14)
Preserved in vinegar, pickled ginger may be red, pink, or light yellow. Eat with sushi.

Straw Mushrooms (22)
Cultivated on rice straw, these dark mushrooms have a "meaty" texture. Buy them tinned or dried. Substitute another variety of tinned mushrooms, if desired.

Taro Root (1)
A potato-like vegetable, taro root has dark, hairy skin and light-coloured flesh. Peel before using. Substitute white potato, if desired.

Water Chestnuts (13)
About the size of walnuts, water chestnuts are a root vegetable with a crisp white flesh. Buy them tinned or fresh. Tinned water chestnuts are peeled. If you buy them fresh, peel before using.

Seasonings and Dried Products

Black Sesame Seed (14)
Sesame seed may be black or white. It is often toasted to enhance the flavour.

Bonito Flakes (7)
Known as katsuo bushi in Japan, bonita flakes are shaved from dried bonita (a member of the mackerel family). Use to make dashi.

Chinese Sausage (1)
This highly flavoured wind-dried sausage is made with pork or liver. Cook before eating. Substitute smoked sausage or dried salami, if desired.

Dashi-No-Moto (8)
This stock base is sold in powdered form. Mix with water and use as an instant substitute for dashi, if desired.

Dried Cloud Ears (13)
Smaller in size and more delicate in flavour than wood ears, these edible fungi absorb flavours from other foods and add a crunchy texture. Soak cloud ears in hot water, then rinse and remove the tough stems before using.

Dried Lily Buds (12)
Sold as tiger-lily buds or golden needles, these dried buds add texture and a delicate flavour to Oriental dishes. Soak in hot water before using.

Dried Mushrooms (18)
Also known as dried black mushrooms or winter mushrooms, these crinkly edible tree fungi add a chewy texture and a smoky flavour to Oriental dishes. The Japanese variety is called shiitaki. Soak mushrooms in hot water, then rinse and remove the tough stems before using.

Dried Red Chilli Peppers (3)
Hot and fiery, dried chilli peppers are popular in many Oriental cuisines. To reduce hotness, remove the seeds before using. Handle with gloved hands for protection from the pepper oils.

Dried Shrimp (10)
Shelled, salted, and sun-dried, these tiny shrimp have a sharp flavour and aroma. The colour may vary. Soak in hot water before using.

12

11

16

13

17

14

10

15

18

Dried Tangerine Peel (16)

Dark brown and brittle, tangerine peel is sun-dried to produce a seasoning with a pungent flavour. Substitute your own home-dried peel (see tip, page 11), if desired.

Dried Wood Ears (17)

Also sold as tree ears, these large edible mushrooms are coarser in texture than cloud ears. Soak in hot water, then remove the tough stems before using.

Five-Spice Powder (6)

This fragrant mix of spices includes cinnamon, star anise, fennel, Szechwan peppers, and cloves. Other spices may be added. Substitute your own homemade blend (see tip, page 11), if desired.

Ground Laos (4)

Laos is the Indonesian name for galangal root, which is a member of the ginger family. More aromatic and delicate in flavour than ginger, laos is sold dried or ground.

Kelp (9)

Called konbu in Japanese, kelp comes from the sea and is used to make dashi. The white powder found on the dried sheets adds a sweet flavour to the stock.

Nori Seaweed (11)

A common seaweed eaten in Japan, nori is used as a sushi wrap. Toast to enhance the flavour before using.

Star Anise (15)

This star-shape spice has a licorice-like flavour and aroma. Substitute 1 teaspoon ground aniseed for one star anise, if desired.

Wasabi Powder (5)

Known as Japanese horseradish, wasabi is unrelated to our horseradish but similar in flavour. Buy the light green powder and mix with water to form a paste. Wasabi is also sold as a paste.

Whole Szechwan Peppers (2)

Reddish brown in colour, these berries produce a slight numbing effect on the tongue. Substitute whole black peppers, if desired.

Sauces and Flavourings

Chilli Oil (17)
Flavoured with chilli peppers, chilli oil adds hotness to Oriental dishes. Substitute your own homemade oil (see tip, page 11), if desired.

Chilli Paste (1)
A fiery condiment, chilli paste varies according to the country of origin. When ground soyabeans are added, it is called hot bean paste.

Chilli Sauce (16)
This tangy, reddish sauce is made with chilli peppers, vinegar, and spices. The ingredients and hotness vary, depending upon the country of origin.

Chinese Black Vinegar (9)
Made from rice, black vinegar is commonly used as a dipping sauce and in the preparation of many seafood dishes. Other common types of rice vinegar are white (clear) and red.

Chinese Soy Sauce (5)
Made from fermented soyabeans, Chinese soy sauce is sold as light (thin), dark (sweetened with caramel), and black (flavoured with black treacle) soy sauce.

Fish Sauce (12)
A thin, salty brown liquid made from salted fish, fish sauce is an indispensable seasoning in Southeast Asia and southern China.

Hoisin Sauce (4)
Thick and rich flavoured, hoisin sauce is made from soyabeans, sugar, garlic, flour, vinegar, and spices.

Japanese Soy Sauce (3)
Made from fermented soyabeans, soy sauce is called shoyu in Japan. It is available in two different types: medium-dark and light.

Mirin (11)
A sweet, syrupy Japanese rice wine, mirin is used in glazes and dipping sauces. Because of its low alcohol content, you'll find it in supermarkets or Oriental food shops, rather than in off-licence stores. Substitute dry sherry, if desired.

Oyster Sauce (14)
A thick brown sauce made from oysters, this sauce is sometimes used by Chinese cooks instead of soy sauce for flavouring food.

Plum Sauce (18)
A thick fruity dipping sauce, plum sauce has a sweet-tart flavour. It is made with plums and/or apricots, chilli peppers, vinegar, sugar, and spices. Substitute your own homemade sauce (see tip, page 11), if desired.

Rice Vinegar (10)
Rice vinegar has a mild, slightly sweet flavour. Chinese rice vinegar is stronger in flavour than Japanese rice vinegar. Substitute white or cider vinegar, if desired.

Rice Wine (8)
Made from fermented rice, rice wine is used as a beverage and for cooking. When it is labelled cooking rice wine, it contains salt and should only be used for cooking. Substitute dry sherry, if desired.

Sake (6)
A flat, colourless Japanese beverage, sake is classified as a beer because of its brewing process. Sake has a high alcohol content and is often served warm for sipping.

Sesame Oil (15)
Thick and aromatic, Chinese sesame oil is made from toasted sesame seed and is golden brown. Because of its strong flavour, it is usually used for flavouring, not for general cooking. Other types of sesame oil are lighter in colour and milder in flavour.

Sesame Paste (19)
Made from ground toasted seed, this thick aromatic paste has a nutty flavour similar to peanut butter. Substitute your own homemade paste (see tip, page 11), if desired.

Shrimp Paste (7)
Available in many forms, shrimp paste is made from fermented shrimp. It has a strong flavour and aroma. Dilute with water before using. Substitute anchovy paste, if desired.

Sweet Soy Sauce (2)
A thick heavy sauce, sweet soy is flavoured with black treacle. Substitute your own homemade sauce (see tip, page 11).

Tamarind Paste (13)
Made from the fruit of the tamarind tree, tamarind paste adds a tart flavour to food.

Nutrition Analysis Chart

U se these analyses to compare nutritional values of different recipes. This information was calculated using Agriculture Handbook Number 8, published by the United States Department of Agriculture, as the primary source. Figures are based on the ingredients used in the American version of each recipe.

In compiling the nutrition analyses, we made the following assumptions:
- For all of the main-dish meat recipes, the nutrition analyses were calculated using weights or measures for cooked meat.

- Garnishes and optional ingredients were not included in the nutrition analyses.
- If a marinade was brushed over a food during cooking, the analysis includes all of the marinade.
- When two ingredient options appear in a recipe, calculations were made using the first one.
- For ingredients of variable weight (such as "2½- to 3-pound [1kg125g to 1kg350g] chicken") or for recipes with a serving range ("Makes 4 to 6 servings"), calculations were based on first figure.

	Per Serving						U.S. Recommended Daily Allowances Per Serving (%)							
	Calories	Protein (g)	Carbohydrate (g)	Fat (g)	Sodium (mg)	Potassium (mg)	Protein	Vitamin A	Vitamin C	Thiamine	Riboflavin	Niacin	Calcium	Iron
Appetizers														
Barbecued Scallops (p. 67)	80	12	6	0	770	340	20	0	0	4	2	6	2	8
Chinese Buns (p. 101)	140	7	20	4	110	150	10	0	0	20	10	10	2	6
Chinese Egg Rolls (p. 99)	120	8	15	3	105	270	10	80	6	8	10	20	0	4
Chinese Roast Pork (p. 10)	60	11	1	2	95	200	15	0	0	25	8	8	0	2
Deep-Fried Phoenix-Tailed Prawns (p. 84)	110	11	10	3	250	130	15	0	0	2	2	10	6	6
Deep-Fried Wontons (p. 89)	40	2	5	2	55	30	2	0	0	4	0	2	0	0
Four-Flavoured Dumplings (p. 96)	50	3	9	1	80	65	4	6	0	6	4	4	0	2
Makizushi (p. 60)	40	2	5	1	190	40	2	8	0	2	2	0	0	2
Moo Shu Pork with Mandarin Pancakes (p. 108)	210	9	16	12	290	210	15	40	4	25	10	10	2	8
Nigirizushi (p. 61)	25	2	4	0	35	25	2	0	0	0	0	2	0	0
Oven-Roasted Spareribs (p. 8)	50	6	4	1	85	115	8	0	0	10	4	4	0	2
Potstickers (p. 100)	60	2	7	2	60	40	4	0	0	8	2	4	0	2
Skewered Pork (p. 100)	60	8	1	3	85	140	10	0	0	30	4	8	0	0
Vietnamese Spring Rolls (p. 92)	40	2	3	2	25	35	2	10	0	2	0	2	0	0
Fillings														
Date Filling (p. 89)	60	1	12	2	0	90	0	0	0	0	0	0	0	0
Peanut Butter Filling (p. 89)	100	4	6	7	65	110	6	0	0	0	0	8	0	2
Pork and Prawn Filling (p. 88)	25	3	1	1	60	45	4	0	0	2	0	2	0	0
Pork Filling (p. 101)	25	2	1	1	25	55	2	0	0	4	2	2	0	0
Sweet Bean-Date Filling (p. 101)	50	1	6	2	0	80	0	0	0	0	0	0	0	0

	Per Serving						U.S. Recommended Daily Allowances Per Serving (%)							
	Calories	Protein (g)	Carbohydrate (g)	Fat (g)	Sodium (mg)	Potassium (mg)	Protein	Vitamin A	Vitamin C	Thiamine	Riboflavin	Niacin	Calcium	Iron
Main Dishes														
Beef and Cabbage Rolls (p. 72)	120	7	2	9	60	135	10	0	7	2	4	6	0	6
Beef and Peppers in Black Bean Sauce (p. 30)	210	24	8	8	1100	430	35	4	60	8	15	25	2	20
Beef and Tomatoes with Fried Noodles (p. 46)	310	21	34	9	480	380	30	10	37	25	15	30	2	20
Cantonese Firepot (p. 53)	310	37	21	8	2080	970	60	70	34	20	25	60	15	30
Cantonese Lemon Chicken (p. 84)	360	31	24	15	540	390	45	4	15	8	10	70	4	10
Chicken and Vegetable One-Pot (p. 50)	230	32	13	5	1010	490	50	60	11	8	15	70	8	20
Chicken in Soy Sauce (p. 10)	170	30	1	5	250	270	45	0	4	4	6	70	0	6
Crispy Szechwan Duck (p. 104)	290	24	12	16	930	430	35	2	9	30	35	35	4	25
Egg Dumplings with Pork (p. 56)	220	15	8	14	790	610	25	100	35	15	20	10	10	20
Fried Rice with Chicken (p. 41)	390	24	41	14	210	270	35	8	6	20	8	40	10	20
Fried Rice with Sausage and Crab (p. 41)	460	18	39	25	820	210	25	10	2	30	10	15	6	15
Indonesian Chicken Saté (p. 66)	130	20	1	4	310	190	30	0	0	2	6	40	0	4
Kung Pao Chicken (p. 32)	340	32	19	14	690	420	50	4	4	10	10	70	2	10
Malaysian Fish with Hot Chilli Sauce (p. 70)	330	31	10	17	220	710	45	90	20	20	10	25	6	8
Marinated Salmon (p. 112)	220	24	2	11	570	430	35	2	0	10	8	0	0	6
Mongolian Firepot (p. 52)	400	29	23	21	1570	730	45	30	24	20	25	50	20	30
Nasi Goreng (p. 40)	410	26	43	15	750	540	40	4	6	50	15	25	6	20
Peking Lamb with Spring Onions (p. 35)	210	24	4	9	470	330	35	0	4	8	10	25	0	10
Pork with Fish Flavour (p. 33)	260	22	12	13	1070	450	35	4	4	30	15	25	2	8
Prawns Saté (p. 67)	160	17	5	9	530	280	25	4	11	2	2	20	6	8
Red-Cooked Beef (p. 111)	210	24	13	7	2120	380	35	0	3	4	10	25	2	20
Red-Cooked Chicken (p. 14)	180	30	4	3	760	300	45	0	0	4	6	70	2	8
Red-Cooked Cornish Game Hens (p. 14)	320	40	20	5	4270	710	60	0	10	10	20	80	6	25
Red-Cooked Young Pigeons (p. 14)	270	31	5	13	1120	490	50	2	0	30	30	60	2	45
Roast Pork with Crispy Noodles (p. 46)	360	29	35	10	400	640	45	4	4	70	30	35	2	15
Steamed Chicken and Vegetables (p. 73)	170	28	6	3	70	500	40	15	18	8	8	60	2	8
Steamed Eggs with Mushrooms (p. 75)	240	16	17	13	230	300	25	20	23	25	20	8	6	10
Stir-Fried Chicken with Noodle Cake (p. 44)	340	26	37	9	750	510	40	160	50	30	20	60	8	15
Sweet and Sour Pork (p. 85)	490	23	42	25	700	620	35	110	110	40	20	25	4	20
Szechwan-Style Pork and Cabbage (p. 34)	180	15	6	11	340	500	25	50	80	30	10	15	10	8
Tempura (p. 82)	310	15	25	15	660	350	25	60	25	10	10	20	6	15
Thai Chicken Saté (p. 64)	250	28	4	14	70	360	40	0	4	4	6	60	2	10
Sauces														
Chilli Oil Dipping Sauce (p. 100)	10	1	1	0	410	35	0	0	0	0	0	0	0	0
Hot Mustard Sauce (p. 10)	30	1	2	2	0	30	0	0	0	0	0	0	2	2
Nuoc Cham (p. 40)	20	0	5	0	105	25	0	4	10	0	0	0	0	0
Peanut Dipping Sauce (p. 64)	80	3	2	7	115	85	4	0	0	0	0	6	0	0

	Per Serving						U.S. Recommended Daily Allowances Per Serving (%)						
	Calories	Protein (g)	Carbohydrate (g)	Fat (g)	Sodium (mg)	Potassium (mg)	Protein	Vitamin A	Vitamin C	Thiamine	Riboflavin	Niacin	Calcium	Iron

Sauces (continued)

Sesame Paste Dip (p. 52)	50	1	2	4	180	45	2	0	0	0	0	2	4	6
Soy-Vinegar Sauce (p. 53)	8	1	1	0	550	45	0	0	0	0	0	0	0	0
Sweet and Sour Sauce (p. 99)	20	0	5	0	130	45	0	0	8	0	0	0	0	0
Sweet Soy Dipping Sauce (p. 72)	4	0	1	0	280	250	0	0	2	0	0	0	0	0
Tempura Dipping Sauce (p. 82)	6	0	1	0	150	10	0	0	0	0	0	0	0	0

Side Dishes

Asparagus in Miso (p. 112)	35	2	4	1	0	210	2	10	35	6	4	4	0	2
Bean Sprouts with Carrots (p. 26)	90	3	11	4	190	280	4	280	15	6	6	4	2	4
Broccoli in Oyster Sauce (p. 24)	90	4	13	4	85	420	6	25	100	4	10	8	4	4
Carrot Salad (p. 112)	25	0	6	0	25	95	0	150	4	0	0	0	0	0
Cucumber Salad (p. 66)	40	0	10	0	70	105	0	4	9	0	0	0	0	0
Kimchi (p. 111)	30	2	5	1	65	280	2	50	52	2	4	2	10	4
Mange Tout with Corn (p. 113)	35	2	5	1	135	90	2	2	25	4	2	0	2	2
Szechwan Stir-Fried Cabbage (p. 26)	70	3	7	4	590	360	4	90	80	2	6	4	10	8
Yangchow Fried Rice (p. 38)	250	14	31	8	660	260	20	4	8	25	6	15	4	15

Soups

Chicken and Vegetable Soup (p. 21)	140	17	12	3	200	490	25	120	15	6	6	30	8	10
Hot and Sour Prawn Soup (p. 20)	110	14	2	5	810	320	20	8	20	0	4	25	4	6
Korean Beef Soup (p. 20)	140	13	6	7	810	420	20	100	8	6	10	20	2	10
Spicy Chicken Soup (p. 18)	260	22	19	10	810	570	35	0	8	8	10	50	4	10
Wonton Soup (p. 88)	140	11	16	3	880	450	15	50	14	15	10	20	6	10

Miscellaneous

Chinese Boiled Rice (p. 38)	110	2	25	0	90	30	2	0	0	•8	0	4	0	4
Dashi (p. 20)	0	0	0	0	0	0	0	0	0	0	0	0	0	0
Fruit Platter (p. 113)	70	1	19	0	0	280	0	30	110	2	4	2	0	2
Lotus Leaf Buns (p. 74)	100	2	15	3	60	50	2	0	0	8	6	6	0	4
Pan-Fried Noodle Cake (p. 44)	170	5	27	4	0	50	6	0	0	20	8	10	0	6
Steamed Orange Roll (p. 75)	130	2	27	2	35	40	2	0	0	2	4	0	0	2
Steamed Silver-Thread Buns (p. 78)	160	3	26	5	95	40	4	2	0	10	8	8	0	8